Praise for *The Sexually* *i*

"Christy Bauman lives with a level of embodiment that is exquisite and rare. From that space she writes with a generosity around her own story that is a lavish gift. Her candor and wisdom around the many aspects of female sexuality are timely and refreshing. You will find yourself drawn in by her stories, and the teaching offered, and left pondering your own stories and how they have shaped your sexuality. This book is a permission giving invitation to explore the "wild edges" of your womanhood and experience a deepened sense of sexual health and joy in your own body."

Tracy Johnson, Red Tent Living

The Sexually Healthy Woman

Essays on Spirituality, Embodiment, and Femininity

Christy Bauman, PhD

DEDICATION

To women whose bodies have been objectified and have not known their body and their sexuality is good, it is.

To Christian women whose church teaching has cost them so much in their sexuality, I pray we can be freed.

To my husband, who has been with me as I deconstruct and reconstruct my sexuality, thank you.

To my daughter, Selah,

and all the daughters in this world,

your body is good.

Table of Contents

Introduction

What is sexual health? Do we actually have a peer-reviewed, healthily researched definition of sexual health? Yes, we do. The Worldwide Health Organization (WHO) currently has eight definitions for sexual health. In a nutshell it is defined as "a state of physical, emotional, mental and social well-being in relation to sexuality and not merely the absence of disease, dysfunction or infirmity" (WHO, 2006).

If you Google the definition of sexual health it is defined as, "the ability to embrace and enjoy one's sexuality throughout one's life." What if you don't know if you have the ability to embrace and enjoy your sexuality? What if you were never taught that your sexual pleasure is important and that your body is good? This book is for you.

This is not a book about beliefs on sexual orientation, these are essays exploring sexuality from the viewpoint of a PhD, highly spiritual, heterosexual, white woman who's sexuality was damaged growing up in the purity culture. Because I can not divorce myself from my experiences, I use them to wrestle with ideas about sexual health. I have also asked a colleague to contribute an essay on sexuality as a woman of color. I wish I would have done more, asked women of all different sexual orientations, spiritual backgrounds, and ethnicities to contribute, and one day, I hope to. Until then, this book is written about my experiences in my personal life and stories from clients in my practice. I follow the guidelines of a Womanist belief system which invites all women's sexuality and the stories of their bodies to the table although its origin is Black women's bodies and stories. This book is not to exclude bisexual, queer, or homosexual women but will be limited due to the scope of the author.

Particularly in the Protestant Christian world, sexuality for me was not explained or unpacked in the lens of spiritual well-being. Luckily, we have a few female Christian sex therapists who have begun to blaze the way, such as Sheila Gregoire. Her book, *The Great Sex Rescue* and Tina Schermer Sellers' book *Sex, God, and the Church* are incredible contributions to sexual health. There are others paving the way, such as Emily Nagoski's *Come As You Are*; *Turning Inward: Essays on Finding God in Female Sexuality* by Christina Marietta, and any of Gina Ogden's research.

So why am I writing this book?

I wrote this book because I am **NOT** a sexually healthy woman. That's right, you heard me correctly. My sexuality was not fostered in a sexually healthy society, and therefore, I have known sexual unhealth. Even moreso, in the Western purity culture, I have been groomed to construct sexuality through a patriarchal, male-interpreted lens. I am very aware that I have spent my entire life absorbing messages about my sexuality rather than constructing them from intuition and honest desire. In Tara Westover's book, *Educated*, she reflects that women have been so impacted by a male-informed world, we will never truly know what a woman is outside of a male-impacted framework. I found this sentiment to be true in my research of female sexuality. Although the female body and arousal cycle holds an undeniable different cadence than that of male sexuality, it is impossible to know what women's desires are without the influence of male impact.

I also wrote this book because my husband wrote a book entitled, The Sexually Healthy Man a few years ago and I have always felt compelled not to allow women's research to be further behind as we live in a patriarchal society. I am writing this book because we cannot have enough Christian women speaking about their experience and understanding of sexual health. For the Christian woman, we fall even further behind in well articulated research on Christian women's sexual health because we are just emerging from decades of purity culture in the white, patriarchal church systems of the Western world. I wrote this book because we need all women's voices bringing their stories to the table. The church needs women of faith sharing an understanding of sexuality and how God sees it. This book may not be for everyone, but if you are a spiritual woman who has not fully integrated herself with her sexual well-being, this book is perfect for you.

I must name my biases first as any good researcher would do; I am an Italian-Lithuanian-French, Christ-following, heterosexual woman. When I speak about sexuality in these essays, my white-ness is the racial construct that will impact the lens from which I write. I was born in 1980 and grew up surrounded by the Bible-belt mentality and purity culture. I received a purity ring from my parents in high school and bought another one for myself in college to "renew my vow" to God. So, there will be a definite particularity to my essays. I am a writer who uses her own story to put words on paper; therefore, this will be more like a memoir than scientific research. I have been a mental health therapist for 15 years and listened to over 800 women tell their stories about sexuality. Of these 800 women, 76% identify as heterosexual and 24% as bisexual, queer, homosexual, or questioning. I bring 10 years of doctoral research into the essays, allowing me to offer what I have found to influence women's well-being in spiritual and sexual health.

Lastly, I include a glossary that defines the relevant terms used in this book. I have asked a few other colleagues and scholars to weigh in about their understanding of Christian female sexuality. Please note this book is not going to cover all aspects of Christian sexuality and it is not intended to, this book is my own experience and therapeutic stories that I want to share to help women break through the sexual roadblocks they have been stuck under within Christianity and sexual health.

I hope this book brings you insight, freedom, and curious exploration of your own sexual health.

Definitions of Relevant Terms

Feminist Identity – Downing and Roush (1985) developed a model of feminist identity development to explain how women may move from a state of passive acceptance of sexism to a greater understanding of the ways in which sexism has affected their lives. The 4 stages are: passive acceptance, revelation, embeddedness-emanation, and synthesis stage. Feminist identity is not a linear process; researchers often assess attitudes associated with these dimensions of feminist identity (Watson et al., 2018).

Feminist Theory – Seeks to understand gender inequality and is the experiences with gender oppression, racism, and sexism (Watson et al., 2018)

Feminist Theology – The study of how women relate to the divine and the world around them as equal creations in the image of God. Longstanding patriarchal oppression and discrimination of women: *critique* of sexist interpretations and practices; *retrieval* of women's past contributions to ecclesial life and theological reflection; interpretations and practices. The idea of referring to God as "mother" or "she" is anathema to many modern Christians. Theological language was in the past much more fluid in terms of gender, frequently referring to God, Christ, and the Holy Spirit in maternal metaphors and symbols. The appeal to inclusive language is seen as masking rather than resolving the problem of androcentrism (Young, 2000).

Misogyny - dislike of, contempt for, or ingrained prejudice against women by both men and women (Nzeyo, 2019).

Objectification Theory (OT) – Posits that girls and women are typically acculturated to internalize an observer's perspective as a primary view of their physical selves (Fredrickson & Roberts, 1997).

Orgasm - the climax of sexual stimulation or activity, when the peak of pleasure is achieved, marked by the release of tension and rhythmic contractions of the perineal muscles, anal sphincter, and pelvic reproductive organs. In women, it is accompanied by contractions of the wall of the outer third of the vagina. (APA, Dictionary of Psychology, 2022).

Patriarchy - a system of society or government in which men hold the power and women are largely excluded from it (Omvedt, 1986).

Patriarchy Stress Disorder (PSD) - defined as the collective inherited trauma of oppression that forms an invisible inner barrier to women's happiness and fulfillment (Rein, 2019).

Resilience – The lack of post-traumatic disorder following trauma (Levine et al., 2009).

Sex - the capacity to derive pleasure from various forms of sexual activity and behavior, particularly from sexual intercourse. All aspects of sexual behavior, including gender identity, orientation, attitudes, and activity. (APA, Dictionary of Psychology, 2022).

Sexual Health - A state of physical, emotional, mental, and social wellbeing in relation to sexuality (WHO, 2002; Edwards et al., 2004).

Sexual Objectification (SO) – Objectification theory (Fredrickson & Roberts, 1997) occurs when a woman's body or body parts are singled out and separated from her as a person and she is viewed primarily as a physical object of male sexual desire (Bartky, 2015; Szymanski et al., 2011).

Sexual Shame – A visceral feeling of humiliation and disgust toward one's own body; identity as a sexual being with a belief of being abnormal, inferior, and unworthy. This feeling can be internalized but also manifests in interpersonal relationships having a negative impact on trust, communication, and physical and emotional intimacy. Sexual shame develops across the lifespan in interactions with interpersonal relationships, one's culture and society, and subsequent critical self-appraisal (a continuous feedback loop). There is also fear and uncertainty related to one's power or right to make decisions, including safety decisions, related to sexual encounters, along with an internalized judgment toward one's own sexual desire (Clark, 2017).

Shame – The belief that there is something wrong with oneself, delineated from guilt, with the belief that there is something wrong with the action (Tangney & Dearing, 2003; Vliet, 2009).

Shame Resilience Theory (SRT) – Proposes that shame resilience, as indicated by location on the shame resilience continuum, is the sum of (a) the ability to recognize and accept personal vulnerability; (b) the level of critical awareness regarding social/cultural expectations and the shame web; and (c) the ability to form relationships to which one feels a belonging (Brene, 2012).

Subjective Well-being (SWB) – Well-being, including happiness, life satisfaction, and positive affect (Diener, 2009).

Womanist Theology – Womanist Theology re-evaluates the roles of women of color among religious settings, reinterpreting male-dominated imagery, sexism, and oppression around the language of God, specifically in matters of career, motherhood, and matriarchal religion (Moradi et al., 2003). The following section of this chapter will include a description and discussion of Womanist Theology which will serve as the theoretical lens for this study.

Womb Theology - Womb theology is the study of God through the lifespan of the female uterus (Bauman, 2020).

PART 1:
THE HISTORIC PROBLEM

The Facts of Life

"Our bodies exist in the present.
To your thinking brain, there is past, present, and future, but to a
traumatized body there is only now."

- Resmaa Menakem, *My Grandmother's Hands*

My eyes are red and teary. My Dad's arm is around me as we sit together on our white, wooden back porch swing. Even though I don't remember this moment in many details, the photo taken by my mom brings back a variety of emotions. The backyard of my family home is staring at me in this image: the swing set, bikes, and pink window shutters framing our two-story clubhouse my dad salvaged last Christmas are all tucked back along the fence line against a wide open field that looks onto houseless fields of pecan groves. Even now that body memory of our family home fills me with a pre-verbal knowing of my life before I could remember. I long to be in its safe familiarity again.

I recall this particular afternoon because it was very ceremonial; all four of us children were taken to the back porch individually to have a conversation about the "facts of life" with my parents. I was only five years old at the time and I was excited to be a part of the grown-up talks that my parents usually had with my older siblings. There was a reason I had been included in this round of conversations: a family friend had been forcing some of the neighborhood kids to let him touch their genitals and my parents had found out about it.

I waited patiently for my older sister and brother to return from their time with my parents and then I was instructed to go outside for my big talk. My parents began the conversation by talking about my body and how no one should ever touch me or ask me to touch them in private areas. That's mostly all I can remember, other than the tears that poured down my young cheeks. I am not sure whether they were tears of shame or sadness, but there were hot, tender, crocodile-size tears.

In her book, *My Grandmother's Hands*, Resmaa Menakem says that "Our bodies exist in the present. To your thinking brain, there is past, present, and future, but to a traumatized body there is only now."

The facts of life conversation is one of the moments in life when growing up is accompanied by a loss of innocence. On that fateful day for me, I was invited into the big kid talks because I innocence had been lost. To this day, I have the photo that captured the day I got the "sex talk". My mom snapped a picture of my dad and me praying after the conversation, and it was over just like that.

That is how the facts of life were introduced to me: as an important conversation about vulnerable body parts and dangerous neighborhood kids. I must say, I am glad my parents had a talk with me at all, but I wish it had been a more regular and frequent topic of conversation. This one-time event made sexuality seem not only vague, but intimidating to broach. Silence gave sexuality more space to be secretive, potentially abusive, and shame-filled.

My children are currently in the same age range I was when I first heard about sex, but our dialogue around it is not limited to one talk on the back porch swing. Following the advice of Dr. Tina Sellers, in our home we try to have 100 one-minute conversations about sex.

The first invitations from my kids were innocent observations at bath time, such as "Look at how cool my penis looks" or "What is this button inside my vagina?"—all of which are invitations to conversations of blessing and protection. Too often we make them conversations of shame. My responses range from blessing to curiosity. "Wasn't God so good to give you a body part that makes you feel good?" or "Why do you think God gave you your penis?"

When children feel safe to ask, the conversations become endless.

The other night before bed, my son and daughter were laughing about the idea of them each having the opposite genitalia. I engaged their imagination as I tucked them into their bunk beds. The playful conversation was light, hilarious at times, and absolutely fascinating to engage. Because I spend most of my work hours as a therapist listening to stories of sexual abuse, I found myself nervous, not sure of what was too much, but I calmed my body and allowed my kids to be theologians.

My daughter explained that her good body button (i.e., her clitoris) was God's way of making her laugh. I laughed out loud, and we talked about the responsibility of our body parts and how to help them live a safe and healthy life with our bodies that God created. This is how we engage the facts of life in our household because these simple facts are filled with complexity and the desperate need for curiosity.

We ended the conversation, shared stories about the day, read, sang, prayed, and I said goodnight. My daughter's words haunted me about her clitoris; she had more trust in God's delight about her sexual body than I did. I began to research the clitoris, a female organ with 8,000 nerve endings and no other physiological function than pleasure. Why am I so puzzled that God gave me a body part that is only there to give me pleasure? The clitoris has more nerve endings than the head of a penis, which has only 4,000 nerve endings. Why would God give women a sexual organ that doesn't impact her ability to have children, it is a body part solely for enjoying? On the other hand, why would evil target the clitoris in female mutilation? Female pleasure has been targeted in multiple ways.

There are few seminaries who are allowing Christ-following students to research and question such theologies of sexuality. While my husband was studying for his Masters at The Seattle School of Theology and Psychology, I would sit in on the sexuality lectures. My mentor, Dr. Dan Allender's words resound in my head. In class a student had asked whether it was Christian to masturbate or not, to which Dan replied, "Of course, as long as you masturbate to the glory of God." The classroom was silent. No one had any words to follow his response, but we all felt freed by his boldness. These are the things Christ-following children should be able to talk to God about when they feel safe. Have you been safe enough to ask these questions? Has God been a safe enough God to answer these questions for you? I want to be a believer who can ask God questions like, "How does one masturbate to the glory of God?" or "Why give women a clitoris with double the nerve-endings than a penis?"

If we return to my children's conversations about male and female genitalia, they are wondering who has the "better" sexual organs. It might be because I am female and partial, but if women have twice the nerve endings as males, maybe women have "better" sexual organs? Or maybe because men's sexual hormones on average last until their 70's surpassing women's sex drive by twenty years, maybe God gave men the sexual upper hand? The freedom to ask these questions are important to sexual health. My children expose the safety they feel to be curious about God's design of their sexual organs, while I feared ever breathing such a thought at their age.

May God become a safe parent in whom we can ask our questions about the facts of life.

Fe(MALE) Sexuality

"Patriarchal Stress Disorder is a collective oppression due to male-interpreted narratives that consciously or unconsciously form barriers to another's self-awareness or fulfillment."

-Dr. Valerie Rein

"I have sex with my husband every week so that he won't go looking elsewhere."

"Yes, he hit me, but he was drunk and high, and he begged me to forgive him and have sex to reconnect, so I did. We have been married for decades but it felt like I was selling myself."

"We have sex about three times a week, but I only have to do that for two more years until I can divorce him and legally get half of our assets."

"Our pastor said to save our marriage and help him with his pornography addiction, I should have sex with him everyday, no matter how I felt."

"Of course I have sex with him anyway, I don't want him to leave me in a double-wide trailer, single-parenting our kids while he re-marries some hot, young girl."

"I told all my kid's they could trust their youth pastor, that he understood the harm of purity culture and women's objectification, and then he started sleeping with my daughter's best friend."

"We had sex the night before he left for a work trip and the night he came home from his work trip, and he still lied to me about going to a strip club the two nights he was gone."

"We only have anal sex, even though it hurts, at least we aren't haven't intercourse and are still virgins."

These are statements I recorded in my therapy notes in one week. One week. It is not uncommon for me to hear such statements from my clients, but the fact that this was in the span of one week made me crawl out of bed before 5am to write this article. I usually sigh deeply when I hear one of my female clients confess something like this about her sex life. I think to myself, *what the hell is wrong with the Christian church that teaches and promotes such a toxic narrative to women?* I tell myself that most women aren't walking around thinking this much about men's sexual desires. Yet, the stories keep coming, women continue, for over fifteen years now, reporting these harmful beliefs about their perceived responsibility to men's sexuality.

And, even I find myself hesitant as I think about my own husband packing his bags and flying to Mexico for a guy's trip later today. We haven't had sex in a month due to our cross-country move, weeks of conflict, 10 days of quarantining with covid, and a hellacious period for me. We fought again last night and there was not an ounce in me that wanted to have sex with him, even though I wouldn't see him for a week. The thoughts began to run like familiar scripts, *he is going to be on the beach around hundreds of women in bikinis, he has been sober for over a decade but things are really hard right now.* Historically in the church, women have been taught to spend more energy thinking about how they look, what they are wearing, and how to protect and satisfy men's sexuality. If I haven't heard it a hundred times, "I didn't want to make him stumble" or "If I wouldn't have sex with him he would have found it somewhere else".

Guess what? Men are grown-ass humans responsible for their own sexuality. Why are we okay being conditioned to tiptoe around men's sexuality when we should be focusing our energy on our own sexual health?

Dr. Valerie Rein explains that Patriarchal Stress Disorder is a "collective oppression due to male-interpreted narratives that consciously or unconsciously form barriers to another's self-awareness or fulfillment".

This means, **if you spend more time thinking about what men think rather than what you think about yourself, you have an oppressed mindset.**

Truthfully, I am so tired of feeling like I am in charge of a man's sexuality. Christian, patriarchal narratives were genius to put the responsibility of men's sexuality on women. Do you think it is common for men to walk around thinking about women's sexuality and their responsibility to keep women sexually satisfied? After sitting through countless therapy hours with married couples over the years, there are only two couples I can remember when the wife complained that her husband wouldn't have sex with her, and those two men didn't seem very convicted or worried at all that their wives were sexually unsatisfied.

The Christian sexual narrative is archaic at best, committing ourselves to sermons about celibacy, abstinence, and *True Love Waits* is not truly teaching anyone about sexual health. The generation that followed those teaching were closet porn users or having anal sex to keep themselves "virgins".

The Law of Onah is the oldest Jewish sexual laws we have but I have yet to hear a Christian couple hear about them before I mention it. The Hebrew words onah (עוֹנָה) is used in Jewish law to refer to a husband's responsibility to satisfy his wife's sexual needs. The Laws of Onah are simple practices of sexuality to help guide a couple, and they claim the female's sexual needs are the ultimate focus, not he male. There is an entire essay later in the book spelling out the Laws of Onah.

When the female's mind gets hijacked by a patriarchal lens, she forfeits her body and her intuition. Sexual health comes when each partner is embodied within themselves and their own desires, and able to share them with each other without manipulation or shame. Sex does not become a weapon in a marriage but a bridge to mutually connect. I believe Christian men are more than horny adolescents. I believe Christian men can become safe, healthy sexual humans who will reclaim the harmful and selfish sexual stance they have created. I believe fe(male) sexuality needs to back their own sexuality as God always intended.

The Construction of Sexual Health

"The spiritualization of sensuality is called love: it is a great triumph over Christianity."

-Friedrich Nietzsche

There are more than 10 of us gathered in her cozy, candle-lit living room on a dark, winter night in Seattle. As progressive as I felt within my church, I have never been to a church-led sexual health class, but luckily, I feel really close to all the women here. All of us have gone to church together for over a decade now and most of these women have seen me naked at some point (skinny-dipping at a women's church retreat) so I feel a little more comfortable coming to a women's sexual health gathering at my friend Cherie's house. She is my pastor's wife, so there is probably no other person I feel safer learning about sex from.

Interestingly enough, all of the women here are over 35 years old and in committed marriages. Even though I can tell you about each of the tear sizes from their births, I am not really sure about the details of their sex lives. It is crazy to me that we know some of the deepest secrets about each other, from our ten years of female friendships to helping each other midwife our children into this

15

world, but I still feel awkward asking them how often they have sex or whether their husbands struggle with pornography. Part of me assumes that my guy friends aren't looking at porn because they are such good men who love women, and then the other part of me assumes they are because isn't that what all men do? These questions still feel taboo with friends I feel comfortable enough having at my births, shooting breast milk at, and skinny dipping with during church retreats, why do I still hesitate to ask questions about sex?

So, I am very excited and nervous to be here tonight, in this living room, about to have honest conversations about sex. I am also excited to not be the one leading this time. It will be nice to receive information, direction, and care from these two women who are leading us. We begin with a welcome and breathing into our bodies. We do a little bit of yoga and stretching before we are asked the question, how would you describe your sexual self? Oh goodness, here we go! These two women always go for the jugular. I am immediately stumped by the question…how WOULD I describe my sexual self? I didn't see that one coming.

Sadly, at 35 years old, I had never been asked that question of myself or my sexuality. I did not grow up to be a very sexual human being. In fact, as a young girl in the church, asexuality was conditioned into me as holiness. I felt afraid that I might fail to answer this question. I was sure I had never explored who my sexual self was.

We were asked to take 10-15 minutes to explore the question. There were sensory tables set up with stations for us to explore how our body feels: a water station, a sand station, a dirt station, an olfactory station, a fire table, and many others. We journal silently for a while, before some of the women get up and awkwardly maneuver their way through the different stations. I am so curious about how my body will respond; I have no idea what I will gravitate toward.

I am patient and kind with myself as I let the different elements touch my skin. It isn't until I get to the water station that I start to feel something. My body actually felt something! The water running over my skin reminded me of growing up snorkeling in the ocean. This sent me back to my teenage years when I would visit my dad in Belize during the summer. We would spend the days out snorkeling for conch and lobster in the ocean. The salt water would buoy me as I gazed for hours through my goggles, looking for conches to gather for homemade ceviche that night. When we would break from our spear fishing, I would always be rewarded with a cold, glass bottle of Coca-Cola from the ice chest. The smooth glass against my snorkel released lips and the sugary cold liquid on my salt-watered mouth is one of the most visceral feelings I can feel. The water and sand from the sensory tables took me back to those moments, where I felt so very alive. The body memory felt so clear, I could feel the weightlessness of my body, the warm sun on my skin, and it felt sensual. I coached myself through the exercise, *Good Christy, you feel your senses and they will lead you to knowing who you are sexually.*

Sensuality is the gateway to sexuality.

Sensuality is defined as the enjoyment, expression, or pursuit of physical, especially sexual, pleasure. However, I could not even start there. I had to go further back; sensuality had to mean enjoyment and expression of my senses: taste, touch, sight, sound, and smell. It was through feeling my senses that I was able to begin to identify my sexual self.

How one defines their sexual self is the roadmap to understanding one's sexual health. Sexual health as we defined in the introduction is a state of physical, emotional, mental and social wellbeing in relation to sexuality. We will need to unpack that some more to actually gain a sense of what sexual health is. Sexual health can be simply defined a sense of well-being and positive affect from one's sexuality.

Here are questions to consider:

When it comes to your sexuality, do you embrace and enjoy your sexuality throughout your life as it refers to well-being, including happiness, life satisfaction, and positive affect?

If you can't answer this, let's try the reverse. Sexual shame has been defined as "a visceral feeling of humiliation and disgust toward one's own body and identity as a sexual being and a belief of being abnormal, inferior, and unworthy" (Clark, 2017). We will dive deeper into the full definition of sexual shame in later essays. Until then, let's use this snippet of the definition to find which characterization you gravitate to more.

When you consider your sexuality, which characterization do you lean towards—sexual health or sexual shame?

Does your sexuality produce positive or negative effects on you?

Begin slowly. Take each question and answer the first response that comes. I call it the "embodied response", the answer you give before you have had too much time to think. As the reader, you will want to begin defining your own definition of sexual health. Depending on your gender, your sexual orientation, your story, your background, and your lived experiences, the definition of sexual health will be able to emerge.

Purity Culture
The Woman in White

"Sexual shame as internalized feelings of
disgust and humiliation
towards one's own body and identity as a sexual being."

-Dr. Noel Clark

This is the dress.

I breathed the words barely above a whisper, just loud enough for my mom and best friend to hear. As I stood in the bridal mirror mesmerized by my reflection, I heard my mom break the awe of the moment with a quick clarifying question: "But we can get this dress in white, right?"

Although the ivory tone of the chiffon looked more expensive to me, I immediately knew why she was asking. It was important for my mother to have her daughter walk down the aisle in white to represent my chastity. Society has long symbolized the purity of the bride with a white dress. In Jewish custom, it is the father of the betrothed who gives an oath of his daughter's virginity, but in Western Christianity, it would be my charismatic Catholic mother who would swear to my virginity with the whitest fabric she could afford.

White. What does a woman in white represent? White has historically been associated with freedom, innocence, omnipotence, and most commonly, purity. Long before the purity movement in Christianity, there was a demand for chastity; an expectation of sexual innocence placed on women that was not expected of men. Women have come to bear the weight of wearing white. Sexism and patriarchy have wielded shame and stigma, demanding a woman's worth be tied to her virginity. These two evil agents of destruction have seeped into the church and ravaged its women. Anyone who allowed herself to be shamed into remaining pure until marriage was promised a happy, healthy sex life, yet psychological research shows us that a significant percentage of couples in marriages from the purity movement are now in couples therapy seeking help with navigating their sexual health.

Sexual shame is the culprit.

Christian men typically grow up learning about sex through hidden pornography use, while Christian women squelch their sexuality, ascribing holiness to a lack of sexual desire. When I asked 400 of my female Christian clients how often they orgasm in heterosexual relationships, they said 10-15% of the time; and when I asked how often their male partners orgasm, the answer was 95-100% of the time. This is called the orgasm gap. Sheila Gregoire's book, *The Great Sex Rescue*, is an incredible book with revolutionary research about the orgasm gap.

Dr. Noel Clark (2017) defines sexual shame as internalized feelings of disgust and humiliation towards one's own body and identity as a sexual being. For church-going women, body image issues and sexual shame have often been narrated through patriarchal theologies. How have we allowed our bodies and our spiritual health to be defined by men? How has shame stolen our healthy, God-intended sexual arousal? Many women who practice patriarchal-based faiths have a skewed understanding of body image and sexuality. Women who identify as lesbian or queer may receive a potential double dose of shame from the pulpit—first, due to their sexual orientation, and secondly, due to body image and general issues related to sexual activity.

On my wedding day, I was the only person wearing white. I felt the need for the color of my dress to symbolize the bride of Christ. My wedding day was everything I dreamed of, short of the cold temperature; but once we cut the cake and someone went to prepare the getaway car, I began to panic. I was crying with my bridesmaids as I changed into my exit dress. My tears were hot as I confessed my fear that losing my virginity might make me less holy in the eyes of God and others.

There is a sexual state that sexual shame from the pulpit also encourages, but it is less often spoken of: asexuality—a lack of sexual attraction. It is very common to hear complaints from my clients of a significant decline in sexual desire after the wedding night. I have heard partner after partner say, "My wife was all over me when we were dating, and now she never wants to have sex." This is not limited to gender, but to couples who used sexual shame as a way to engage their sexual development before marriage.

That was my story, too. The safety of dating meant I could do everything except have sex. I felt safe to explore my arousal because I knew we would never consummate it until the wedding night. Upon the arrival of the wedding night, my sexuality shifted. It has taken eleven years of marriage and therapy for me to approach sex differently, with uninterrupted eye contact with my partner and a curiosity towards my own body and pleasure, rather than my focus being only on my partner's arousal.

Every day in my counseling practice, I witness clients attempting to untangle their sexual shame. Abuse is a huge part of the work I do in my counseling practice, and I often remark that abuse can be absorbed by nature, which is why I use nature in therapy. Yet there is something about sexual shame and sexual trauma that is lodged deep into the body, and nature has yet to expunge it. Sexuality is so embodied with sensuality. Therefore sexual trauma, whether spiritual, physical, emotional, or mental is so difficult to untangle from body. Our arousal cycle does not flourish in places of shame. Many of us continue to feel shame or lack of desire within the covenant.

May our sexuality become a powerful prayer, an act of spiritual revolution. Who taught you to believe God ever meant for us to be dressed all in white? Purity has been used as a dangerous measurement that God never intended to be a judgement of our sexuality.

Leaving My Father's House

"Fathers, be good to your daughters, for daughters will love like you do. Girls become lovers who turn into mothers; so mothers be good to your daughters too."

-John Mayer, *Daughters*

I open the door from the bridal suite; my bridesmaids are behind me. My father's face, which mirrors mine so much in resemblance, is staring at me. He takes my arm and places it under his broad shoulder, before we move to turn toward the wedding aisle, he looks at me pleadingly. "You don't have to do this if you don't want to, Christy." I laughed and brushed off my father's jaded invitation as if it were a joke. He is not speaking this warning because he thinks my husband is a poor choice for partnership; he says it because he has never believed in marriages working out. My father knows little of keeping a marriage together. The number of women who have been a part of his story is more than I can count. When it comes to understanding sexual health, being my father's daughter has been hellish at best. Those of us who are born to a womanizing father have a long road of repairs to make in our relationships with men. Men who buy into a culture that objectifies women raise girls with distorted self-esteem. I am reminded of the lyrics in John Mayer's song, "Daughters": "*Fathers, be good to your daughters, for daughters will love like you do.*"

Western Christianity has not helped me heal from men's objectification of women; it has confused me at best. Through psychological lenses, I have come to see my heavenly Father as a good God who is not like my biological father. Father God has loved me differently, and He has required me to leave my earthly father's house. Some interpret scripture as commanding women to stay under a headship their entire lives and this left me feeling defiant and somewhat defeated. The historical context of women in the Bible leads me to believe that I was supposed to be under my father's headship, a husband's headship, or a pastor's headship. Personally, I wanted to know more because I had not known many good men in my story as healthy stewards of their own sexual health let alone other women's sexual health.

As I dug further into Biblical and psychological research, I realized God longed for women to be protected and provided for, in a sense, covered by God, the Father; God, the Husband. Because my personal experiences involved men who did not portray attributes of God, it skewed my reading of Scriptural protection for women. God sent His Son Jesus to die on our behalf, so the scripture in Ephesians which reads, "Husbands lay down your life for your wife, as Christ laid down His life for the church" (Ephesians 5:25) does not invite women into a patriarchal headship, but a

Christ-like relationship. Too often, I see wives laying down their lives for their husbands, when it is the husband commanded to. There are plenty of church platforms that argue headship beliefs such as complementarian, which specifies the husband and wife roles are complementarian. Or the egalitarian relationship which believes the husband and wife are equals. Spiritual trauma from sexism in the church sets us up to struggle with healthy intimacy and beliefs of equality within Christian women and men.

John Mayer's song continues with this conclusion, "*…but boys would be gone without the warmth from a woman's good, good heart.*" In short, how we leave our father's house impacts how we enter our husband's hearts. When I chose my husband, I had little understanding of my father's impact on my ability to love him. Until I began to work around my hatred of misogyny and objectifying culture, I began to realize the lack of ability I had to engage in healthy intimacy with men. I did not know the impact men had had on my life. Do women know the work of leaving their father's house? Do women think about the act of being passed from one dominant covering to another? Did I imagine the balancing act of being called to lay down my life in a marriage covenant after being raised in a patriarchal culture? No one told me the work of individuation and self-awareness so that I might enter the sacrament of marriage without the PTSD of misogynistic culture.

Take a moment to reflect on these questions:

How many good men do I know in my life?

Do I believe I have emotionally left my father's house?

Do I have PTSD from the impact of an objectifying culture?

How has my relationship with men affected my relationship with healthy intimacy?

My Brown Body

Written by Sandhya Oaks

Thank you Sandhya for sharing so vulnerable your experience as a woman of color. I long for all women of color to share their voices around sexual health.

Thank you Sandhya for sharing so vulnerable your experience as a woman of color. I long for all women of color to share their voices around sexual health.

My brown body holds wounds, reminisces of survival, and history of the Caste System.

My dark ashy knees hold mockery and disgust.

My skin color holds isolation.

Middle school is rough for so many reasons. Gym class was particularly crude. These are the years when you need to change clothes before class. Gray or black shorts and white t-shirts were the non-optional style. Let's be real, no one looks good in gray cotton shorts. And after a few weeks, the loose pure white cotton shirts will soon take on the pale yellow stains of adolescent markings from the 50 minute class time of running around.

Our class was playing a game that divided us into two teams. We were in the middle of the game and all seemed well in the world of a noisy fifth grade gym. I remember exactly where I was standing in the gym when some girls on the other team drew attention to my body. One girl looking and pointing at my knees said in a loud tone, "look at your knees, they are so dirty...do you not know how to wash yourself?". I looked down in panic and saw my ashy black knees and by the time I looked up I saw the other few girls staring at me, joining in with faces of disgust. I felt gross. I felt exposed. I felt small. I wanted to hide my knees and my entire being. I looked around the gym trying to find someone else who also had darker knees like mine, and I came up empty in a gym full of white, pale, pasty legs. I was the only one with brown skin in the class, and I had no one to mirror my dark knees. I wanted to know I wasn't alone and that this claim of being unclean would wash away. I still recall the heaviness of shame that followed me into the girls locker room after class. I was still in the depths of "unclean" and now needed to strip off my clothing and change back into my non-gym clothes...again, in a locker room filled with other fifth grade girl bodies that didn't look like mine. I did the crouching, toss your normal clothes on top of your gym clothes, pull off your gym clothes like a magic trick move and fought to keep as much of my brown skin covered as possible. I left the locker room and moved into the rest of my day, dreading that I still had to make it through a few more classes before the end of the school day came.

When I got home, I made a sprint to the bathroom, locked the door and stared into the mirror at my brown face and brown body. The look on my face was that of a young girl searching for the girl in the mirror to bring comfort and balm to the still open and tender wound. I felt ambivalence surging through my whole being. I wanted to look and inspect my body and the darker features it held and part of me wanted to escape with trepidation and turn away from what I might see. I unbuttoned the top bottom of my pants and pulled them down to my ankles to examine my knees. Sure enough I saw what the white girls saw in gym class and felt the shame accelerate inside of me. "How could this be" I thought? I know how to shower and clean myself. I turned around away from the mirror and moved towards the bathtub with my pants still at my ankles. I leaned over the tub to grab a bar of soap and the wash cloth that was hanging above it. I turned on the bathtub faucet, wet the rag and let the water rush over the half used bar of Irish Spring soap. I sat down on the edge of the tub, then scrubbed the bar of soap over the wet dripping rag. Slowly I began to rub the rag over my knee. With little patience, I began to rub with more of a firm pressure and aggression. I wanted the black ashy layer to come off of me. And to be fully honest, I wanted all of the brownness of every inch of my body to be washed off so I could look like everyone else, and deep down inside, feel pretty like the others. I scrubbed and scrubbed and then moved to the other knee to see if I would have different results. I didn't. I couldn't get my knees to be lighter and now they were both reddened by my scrubbing. Why did I have darker knees? I felt so much confusion and grief. I hated my darker features and this bled into hating my brown body. I wanted to have *clean white* skin and be like the other gals. I hated that I couldn't change this part of me and felt stuck.

From this moment on, as I took showers and cleaned myself I took extra time scrubbing my darker elbows and knees trying to scrub away the lie that I didn't know how to properly clean myself. I wore way too much pear scented body spray and became hyper vigilant, terrified of hearing the accusations of "unclean and dirty" again. I never told my parents about what happened or talked about it with others. How could I? Everyone in my family and at school had white clean skin. There was no one to mirror me and help me see otherwise. The pain of holding this "dirty" secret was riddled with shame and contempt.

It wasn't until I was out of college that I began to understand and live into more of my ethnic identity as an Indian Punjabi and Pakistani woman. I focused much of my learning around Indian women and every glimpse I got of one in person, I made sure to study her moves, mannerisms, countenance and of course scanned her body to see if hers looked like mine. When you don't grow up with a racial mirror, one can't help themselves but to search and scan. It's a nature of habit. Unfortunately, most of the Indian women I saw had their knees and elbows covered either because it was the dead of cold midwest winter, or because they were traditionally dressed and honoring the Indian culture of covering their legs.

As I was on my journey of exploring and discovering who I am and where I come from, I simultaneously began to learn about the power of kindness and its ability to disrupt shame. Gentleness was an old word in my vocabulary but new in terms of living it out. My dark black ashy knees were still masked in the comments of the girls in my fifth grade gym class and were in need of care and gentleness. One day, as I stepped out of the shower I took lotion and began going through my typical ritual of covering my body with the shea butter silky-like formula. As I massaged the lotion into my knees, I paused, leaned forward and puckered my lips while letting them gently touch my skin. I moved my head back slowly and looked at my knees. They held a new charming-like sense of beauty and tenderness. I also held a new sense of care for this part of me. I repeated the same ritual on my other knee. I don't know where I learned this from, but I attribute it to being born a nurturer with motherly instincts. This small gesture and gift I gave myself has undone much of the sting that evolved from the lies of being named as dirty. It has helped me to approach myself, my darker features, and my brown body with compassion, honor, and love.

A few summers ago, as I did some reclamation work around the trauma my brown female body has absorbed. I felt led towards creating another ritual to mark the fresh healing my body was experiencing. I invited some friends to meet me at the nearby reservoir and shared my truth of the war that has come up against my feminine brown body. These people bore witness to my pain and lamented alongside me. A couple of friends joined me in the lake and dipped me below the water's edge and back up out. The water was not used to cleanse away my brownness, or dark ashy spots, like I so desperately wanted as a young adolescent girl, but rather as a symbol of renewal in making all things new.

My brown body beholds goodness.

My dark ashy knees behold glory.

My skin color beholds stunning beauty.

I Bless my Beautiful Brown Indian Feminine Body.

Objectification
Gray Matter & Gold Dust

Originally published in Theology of the Womb

"Husbands lay down your life for your wife, as Christ laid down His life for the church"

- Ephesians 5:25, NIV Bible

I woke up one night after a jarring dream. I was watching a man masturbate as he looked at pornography on a computer screen. There was gray ash-like matter coming from his moving hand and drifting into the air, much like fog from pollution. I was suspended into the atmosphere as I watched the gray matter slough off of houses all through the city. The gray matter filled the atmosphere like smog in a major industrial city. I became aware that women all over the world were breathing in this toxic haze, and it was making them sick. I am suffocating from the claustrophobic pollution, waiting for a call from my husband to tell me where to go to find safety from it. There are men looking for me, and I know they are trying to find and rape me. My husband finally calls, and through the broken-up reception he explains that the gray matter is killing women everywhere. It fills their lungs and their bodies, and they are dying. I hear the men who are chasing me getting closer and I start running. My husband tells me that he will never see me again but that I must run to the forest's edge where my sister is waiting to drive us across the border. I run, but before I can make it to her, I am captured by the men and raped to my death.

Whew. Take a deep breath. It was a sobering and intense dream.

Because I work with women who are partnered with sex addicts, this dream is not something out of the blue. Thankfully, I have had some training in dream analysis, and as a therapist who works with healthy sexuality and married to a therapist who works with men in sexual addiction, I know a bit about how to navigate this dream. I woke up and wrote for hours after I had this particular dream. Evil felt very near. The dream's narrative speaks to why I believe we as Christians absolutely must understand sexuality. God created sexuality with power in mind—power for good. Evil has had other ideas of how to use sexuality for harm, hate, and darkness. Sexual assault, rape, and incest are prevalent in our world. One out of every three women has been sexually abused.[1] *Evil would not be running rampant with sexual harm if it weren't just as powerful a weapon for good.* Again, evil would not have the ability to do so much harm with sexuality if God had not created it with the intent of empowerment.

---

[1] Mennicke, A., Anderson, D., Oehme, K., & Kennedy, S. (2014). Law enforcement officers' perception of rape and rape victims: A multimethod study. *Violence and Victims, 29*(5), 814-827.

Would God have created sex if He had known how much pain and harm it would bring? Our Creator had a plan, and a good one, when he designed sex.

For weeks after this encounter, I pondered my dream and what could combat this "gray matter" from sexual harm, if indeed it were poisoning us. I spent a few weeks reading peer reviewed research on the effects of pornography on women's sexuality and health. There is cause to believe the effects of an objectifying society can be seen in the deterioration of women and their health.[2] How could we stop this? What counteracts this destructive gray matter? My answer is holy intimacy and sex, or what I call gold dust.

Intimacy: Gold Dust

I want to take you now to a small corner in North Seattle, 90th and Aurora Avenue to be exact, where my church runs a neighborhood ministry for sexually trafficked women. These are women who spend their lives selling sex for money, food, and drugs. You can imagine the sexual harm and trauma these women have endured and witnessed. I am friends with some of these women. I spend time with them every first Wednesday of the month, and they teach me about God in more ways than I ever imagined. They teach

---

[2] Flood, M. (2009). The harms of pornography exposure among children and young people. *Child Abuse Review: Journal of the British Association for the Study and Prevention of Child Abuse and Neglect, 18*(6), 384-400.

me about hope and resilience, but even more they teach me about what combats this gray matter of sexual harm.

Gold dust is the term I have given to what I believe is produced when someone engages in sexual health. Sexuality is objectified in society and shamed and/or silenced in the Christian world. As believers, we must learn the power of holy and healthy sexuality. Pope John Paul II wrote an entire book on the subject, *The Theology of the Body: Human Love in the Divine Plan*, in which he states:

> "Man thus ceases to live as a person and a subject. Regardless of all intentions and declarations to the contrary, he becomes merely an object. This neo-Manichaean culture has led, for example, to human sexuality being regarded more as an area for manipulation and exploitation than as the basis of that primordial wonder which led Adam on the morning of creation to exclaim before Eve: 'This at last is bone of my bones and flesh of my flesh' (Gen. 2:23). This same wonder is echoed in the words of the Song of Solomon: 'You have ravished my heart, my sister, my bride; you have ravished my heart with a glance of your eyes' (Song 4:9)."

Good sex, life-giving sex, emits a gold dust into the air. Of course, there is no scientific research affirming the existence of gray matter or gold dust, but the imagery is potent. I often recall my seminary professors' question: What is God's design for sexuality? It can't only be reproduction; otherwise, He would never have given women a clitoris. It has to do with pleasure, and I believe that pleasure has a spiritual power. As I pondered these concepts, I eventually began to envision that gold dust could dissipate the gray matter. It took me twelve years of research to answer my professor's question. I believe God created and intended sexuality to defeat evil.

Gold dust is life. Gray matter is death.

PART 2:
My Belief About My Body

Good Breast, Bad Breast

"The first "object" in someone is usually an internalized image of one's mother. The breast that feeds the hungry infant is the "good breast", while a hungry infant that finds no breast is in relation to the "bad breast"."

- Melanie Klein

"Good breast, bad breast." My professor began the lecture.

I wasn't surprised at the term being that we were steeped in our second week of object relations theory at graduate school. Now having had kids and nursing all three of my children, I think back on this theory with such a different vantage point. The theory states that a mother's attachment style with her infant impacts the child's personality in adulthood. Let me just tell you how stressful it is, as a mother, to think your kid's entire future is contingent on your stability and attachment with them. And all of this is during a time where your body is flooded with pregnancy and post-partum hormones. There are a few things I will have to talk to God about at some point. But anyway, you get the idea that the main caretaker is the "object" directly correlated with how the baby will grow up to see the world.

Good breast, bad breast is the concept that most children's first object of attachment is their mother's breast. A child's source of nourishment and comfort is found in the breast. If the breast offers satiating milk, it is considered a good breast. If the breast withholds comfort or sustenance from the child, it is the bad breast.

If you want more context to how this theory came about, here is a short summary. Object relations theory is a psychological standpoint which emphasizes people's adult personalities are impacted by family of origin experiences during infancy. For example, if a person experienced neglect or abuse during childhood from their main caregiver they will assume harmful behavior from anyone who reminds them of the abusive or negligeant caregiver. This theory states that these experiences turn into objects in the unconscious that we all carry into adulthood and use as predictors of behaviors in our social relationships and interactions. Stay with me here, positive interactions with one's caregiver creates expected positive interactions within our adult relationships. Negative interactions with our caregivers impact our brains to expect negative interactions within adult relationships.

Klein states, "The first "object" in someone is usually an internalized image of one's mother. Internal objects are formed by the patterns in one's experience of being taken care of as a baby, which may or may not be accurate representations of the actual, external caretakers. Later experiences can reshape these early patterns, but objects often continue to exert a strong influence throughout life. The breast that feeds the hungry infant is the "good breast", while a hungry infant that finds no breast is in relation to the "bad breast".

I often use this concept with clients to help increase one's ability to tolerate ambiguity, to understand that both the "good" and the "bad" breasts are a part of the same mother.

Many psychotherapists would go on to expound on this theory that if we can continue to hold the good and bad coexist in our caregivers we would less likely turn on ourselves. For example, the therapist offers a child the opportunity to find a new parent, but the child refuses. The therapist asks, "do you want to keep the mommy that broke your arm?" To which the child responds, "yes, it is my fault I hurt my arm".

Clearly, the child must turn on themselves to keep from incriminating the one they love or have come to rely on. If we do not work to expand our ability to hold both the good and bad in every person, we either split ourselves off or we project onto someone else.

As I have worked with hundreds of men and women, there is often a similar "good breast, bad breast" phenomenon going on between genders. We each have a relationship with our mother's breast being offered or withheld from us. This foundational experience invites us to look for our individual relationship with breasts.

Within the sexual construct, there are genderized impacts. Often the genders are both uncertain how to wield and yield this concept both good and bad within their sexuality. For example, the female both loves and hates the power and impotence of her breast, and the man similarly loves and hates his relationship with the female breast due to its ability to offer or refuse him.

Sexuality holds power, with which, women or men are continually exchanging back and forther in relationship.

The women's breasts have power to allure while they also can both give sustenance and withhold it. The female is left to hold the ambiguity that her breasts are both powerful and impotent at times. Take for example, breast that are engorged while nursing, versus flattened breast during a mammogram. She must be careful that if she can not hold this tension, she will be tempted to turn on herself, and thus, on her own breast. This plays out with all women's sexual organs, not only the breast. The female sexual body has the potential to withhold or satiate, the ability to be seen as both "good" and "bad", in relationship with their children, their partners, and themselves.

Due to the dissonance within an objectifying system, the breast has easily become a marketing object that demands us to stretch our capacity to not turn on the female breast. In medical venues, breast health should be focused on bra seams with positive blood flow and lactation health rather than size and augmentation for cosmetic reasons. Millions of dollars go to breast reconstruction surgery rather than lactation health. Without ascribing judgement, what does this mean about our healthcare for women's breast? To be clear, this is not judgment women who spend thousands of dollars on breast reconstruction, or decreasing or increasing her breast size for medical or cosmetic reasons. I bring up the financial discrepancy to illuminate where society focuses their gaze.

Breast health is geared toward the image of a breast rather than the health of a woman. So, may you begin to ask yourself these questions about your breast:

What is your relationship with your mother's breast?

If you were adopted or orphaned, how do you feel about not being breastfed?

Are the size of your brest disappointing or do you favor them?

Do you believe your breast to be both good and bad?

For whose sake do you augment your breast?

These are just the beginning questions to living a life with a healthy breast. Unfortunately, patriarchy has made breasts an object for consumption, therefore, women never have a chance to know what they want without having been influenced by the male view of breasts. Dr. Valerie Rein definies patriarchy stress disorder in laymen's terms as, "an environment where one does not feel free to be themselves". Many women fixate about the size of their breast because there has been power attributed to breast size. When I sit with women in therapy, many deliberate about the mental war they have with their breast: size, shape, sag, etc. all the while not realizing this is not a reflection of good breast, bad breast anymore rather we have just entered their world influenced by patriarchy stress disorder. Men or motherhood have set the lens for breast. The latin origin of breast is satiation, but not in regards to men or mothering.

We must ask ourselves, do my breast satiate me?

If you can answer that question, we can move to the next question.

Do I believe them to be good, bad or both?

If we return to object relations theory of good breast, mad breast. Applying the psychological construct of this working theory of Good Breast, Mad Breast to those who have been impacted by objectification and patriarchal cultures, women must grow their ambiguity with their breast, and ultimately our sexuality, holding both its glory and anger, lest we live our lives disassociated and projecting.

The Female Body Keeps Score

"The amygdala stores the emotional significance
of the traumatic event
as experienced by our five senses."

- Van Der Kolk, The Body Keeps Score

"Okay Christy, here is a warm gown to change into. Everything from the waist up needs to be taken off and I will come get you when it's time for your mammogram imaging. Also, I just wanted to let you know that this is a recall from my first mammogram three weeks ago about something that might be abnormal. We should be able to find out in this appointment if there is something wrong?"

If my grandfather hadn't passed away in the three weeks between these two appointments I might have been more snarky in response to the stress a woman wrestles with during three weeks of no answers except "abnormal" to her first mammogram.

Somehow the work and grief of my grandfather's death distracted me from my fear, but now, at the follow up appointment, undressing behind the curtain of the small, telephone booth like changing room, I felt every anxious thought flood my body.

As she leads me to the mammogram machine, I am grateful that she is extra kind as she aligns my right breast and takes photos. She pauses in front of her computer screen and stares at the images and then asks me if I'm willing to wait while she talks to the radiologist to confirm the discrepancy.

What can anyone answer to such a question, other than, "yes"?

As someone who reads faces I want to ask for clarification of her gaze at the images, or even just choke out, "is something really troubling?".

Instead I squeak out "yes" and she disappears quickly out the door. I am left there in the cold imaging room tending to my sore, recently squashed breast. I sneak around to see four massive black computer screens displaying multiple beautiful images of my right breast. I try to keep my untrained eye from looking at the images for abnormalities. Although I am a mental health therapist, in my internship in the oncology unit over a decade ago, I spent hours in medical rounds and meetings looking at these mammogram images noting traumatized tissue lines for reconstructive breast surgery. But standing here now as my own doctor, my diagnostic skills seem novice at best.

In hopes of not spiraling, I send a text out to my girlfriends telling them where I am along with a picture of my mammogram images. After I press send, I attempt to re-engage the computer screens as a woman trying to see her body rather than analyze it. The screens portray images of electric blue jellyfish strands that make up the tissue in my breast. I am in awe. I can't stop looking at the gorgeous images. What I realize is that the image of my breast, though looking plump and outlined like a perfect rainbow, is actually squished flat on a glass.

This image that I see reflecting back to me, is actually a mirage of perfection, in reality it is an angry, flattened image. The words "mad breast" came to mind. I could see the electric blue sperm like images being smashed. In a moment, I feel a culmination of the discomfort of the procedures, the fear of a lumpectomy or mastectomy, and the weeks of wondering what my prognosis was…my breast were mad. My breasts were not happy at all as this deceptive image portrayed.

All the invisible feelings of female oppression came into focus and I realized the image of female health and women's care looks beautiful on the screen but actually the woman's experience is not being seen at all. Sure, this mammogram is allowing me to see if there are any masses in my breast, but the way in which I am being cared for is not as kind as it looks.

If we use the culture of objectification with this same metaphor, the female's actual sexual experience is very different the than images portrayed on advertising media such as Victoria Secret commercials. The female body appears beautiful and glorified on the societal billboard, yet when we actually take into the female experience her most vulnerable parts are being adjusted and manipulated to offer an image of perfection.

Just like we are able to see trauma in breast tissue where there has been severing, we also know the body remembers trauma through the five senses. In his book, The Body Keeps The Score, Dr. Van Der Kolk provides overwhelming research that **the body holds trauma memory within the five senses**. "The memory of the traumatic event is stored in the amygdala, which ensures you do not find yourself in this dangerous situation again. However, the amygdala doesn't save the event as if it was a story – the amygdala stores the emotional significance of the traumatic event as experienced by our five senses."

This is revolutionary news for the female's sexuality in regards to the trauma of sexual objectification. For many women, no more do we have to wonder why we felt sexually aroused during dating and then lost our sex drive after marriage. The female arousal cycle is impacted by her body's sexual story. As a 15 year mental health therapist and researcher of women's sexual and spiritual well-being, I have seen **that the female body keeps score**. And in the words of my own sex certified therapist, "the brain is the largest sexual organ, therefore if there is trauma affecting our brains, our largest sexual organ is unhealthy".

Women come into my office every week looking like a dolled up version of themselves yet when we uncover the story of their hearts, we find the scars of sexual harm from an objectifying and oppressive society. Women will never be known outside of men's framework, because men have always been here prior to women, setting the precedence.

Men who are able to be aware and curious of this realization allows women their best chance at offering themselves honestly in heterosexual relationships. Often women's worth has been sold to us as their physical beauty rather than their true well-being. As women we must be honest about our felt experience rather than the image we have been conditioned to portray.

Because we don't have clear parameters of sexual harm's effect on sexual health, we must use physiological statistics along with mental health statistics on sexual trauma and abuse to piece together our path to sexual health. For example, although sexual health is not defined by orgasm, the orgasm gap statistically shows women only orgasming at most 50% of the times they have intercourse while men report orgasming 90% of the time, giving us evidence there is a deficit in female sexual health (Gregorie, 2021). The deficit in women's sexual health allows us to deduce a pathway to healthy female sexuality. I believe we can build the road map to women's sexual health in the body's lived experience because the female body keeps score. I invite you the reader, to take a moment to use these categories to begin the exploration to your own sexual health.

When the female is given the opportunity

1. **to tell her story,**

2. **track her sexual development,**

3. **become educated on the effects of objectification,**

4. **and study her arousal cycle,**

5. **understand her sexuality is good.**

we can free the female sexual body and mind. And in turn, we can find our way back to the sexually healthy woman.

Her Body & Her Blood

"Her cycle is reminding us that life only continues
through the life/death/life cycle."

-Dr. Bauman, Theology of the Womb

*"This cup is My blood, My new covenant with you, each time you drink this
cup, remember Me."*

It's been a long week. Come to think of it, it's been a long
couple of years with Covid-19 hitting Seattle by force. We have
stayed home, stopped going to school, changed our work schedules
and so when I find myself eating tablespoons of Nutella from the
jar, I am not super hard on myself. My relationship with food is
always telling me something about how I am doing internally. I
always try to listen to what my body is saying, I become curious
instead of judgmental when I am PMSing: often I have no desire for
sex, ambivalence with the big things, frustration with the small
things, bloating, and a lack of care about exercise or sugar intake.
What I love about when my period comes, **I get really honest**. I
actually say and produce my best work during my bleeding, because
I care less and I become clearer.

Historically, female bleeding has been shamed and hidden, in my book Theology of the Womb, I walk through the history of bleeding and the culture power of the red tent. Women's blood is a gift from God, an invitation to create from their entire being. The act of bleeding is integral to birthing, but not just birthing babies, rather it is the secret to birthing creation. There are four categories my bleeding body has invited me to understand:

1. **The woman's uterus instinctively knows how to birth.**

A woman's body, despite whether she has ever physically birthed, knows how to birth. A body containing a uterus which practices monthly for most of her life to "birth." My body is whispering or yelling truths to me whenever I start to prepare for "birthing". What is my period birthing this time around?

An anxious month,

a celebratory season,

another loss,

a breakup with a lover,

a reckoning with myself?

Whatever the "birth", I can always feel the preparation in my body, building up and waiting to release. I keep looking for blood to come, waiting for relief that these feelings building inside of me will birth something. With every period, my body creates something new each cycle: an honest conversation with my partner, a new idea, a more honest vision of the future, or a big change in life. If I believe my body to be good, I begin to listen to her, and she becomes a trusted friend.

2. **Our body was meant to be a trusted friend; if it isn't, we must mend the trust.**

There is a ***trusted friendship*** that I want to have with my body; *a knowing* that we care for each other; a security that we've got each other's back. In other words, you could ask yourself, *what is my attachment style with my body, how do I engage it?* It is in the moments of disconnect with my body that I feel most alone and out of sorts in the world. It reminds me of what women with a disease have explained as *the* "betrayal" they feel from their bodies, somehow betrayed by a disease that could kill them all the while their exterior looks healthy. I have known this "betrayal" within my body when it has carried a lifeless child within my womb while acting as if all were normal and well. Sometimes, in the everyday monthly cycles of menstruation, I feel a fraction of this PTSD, like my mood, my cramps, my blood are saying something and I want to run from its untrustworthiness, rather than be curious as I would be to hear from a trusted friend. My PMS is an invitation to know myself better.

3. **Cyclical bleeding is an invitation to knowing yourself more.**

These repeated months over a span of almost 40 years are still invitations to knowing myself anew. After being done with pregnancies, I am noticing a new pattern in the week before my pre-menopausal period. It is as if each time I am preparing to birth something, a physical prompting to allow myself to release and shed blood. It feels closer the concept of death and burying, which makes me more vulnerable than I would like to be. Yet each cycle, I am being invited into the act of burying better than the time before. For example, if a woman is embodied her cyclical bleeding is a guide to becoming a death doula. I will not go into this concept very much in this book, but in my book, Theology of the Womb, there is evidence to how our cyclical bleeding teaches the female the importance of her work with burial and death.

For this essay, we will focus on what we can learn from the relief when blood finally after PMS. These days, my bleeding, seems like an explanation and expression to my internal turmoil; I even find myself overjoyed. In the last three months, when blood comes, I run into the other room to tell my husband in some sort of excitement. Like, "See, I knew something was up" or "I did it, I birthed another small hardship through this body of mine." My excitement doesn't make much sense, but ever since the shame of bleeding has been taken away and the stigma of my period has been removed, I feel free to be curious. What is my body trying to birth each month? It actually becomes a wonder that I start to follow its lead and I listen.

4. Approach your bleeding body with shamelessness and curiosity.

In very few cultures would women find blood in their underwear and feel excitement or curiosity. Even if women can overcome the oppression from a patriarchal culture, they don't often look at their own bleeding as a superpower to creativity. Through research and years of therapy, I have reclaimed my female bleeding, hormonal cycles, and my retracting and expanding body. My bleeding is an incredible wonder who I want to not only know, but trust, and even moreso, lead with. When blood comes, I think I can hear my body saying, whispering or yelling,

> *"Come on rise up,*
>
> *come on rise up,*
>
> *come on rise up,*
>
> *come on rise up."*

5. Our blood is saying something to you: "Come on, rise up, this cup is my blood, a new covenant."

May we all be invited into our bleeding as a way of knowing that our bodies are good and our bodies can metabolize the life/death/life cycle. The life/death/life cycle is the concept found in the fruit tree's cycle of the seed, plant, and fruit; in the cycle of the season of fall, winter, spring, and summer; in the story of Christ's life, crucifixion, and resurrection. The cycle of life/death/and life also shows up in the female menstrual cycle.

Like any other cycle in nature, the female cycle follows seasons. Imagine the typical 28 day cycle, as four seasons each lasting 7 days. Every month the female is hormonally living through spring, summer, fall, and winter. Our sexual arousal often mimics these seasons, and may feel more aroused in the spring and summer weeks than in the fall and winter weeks. The female cycle is reminding us that sexual life only continues through the life/death/life phases. We should stop and listen to our wise bodies, for they can teach us so very much. If I listen in these moments, to the God within my body, my uterus shedding its lining and pouring itself out, I hear Her speaking.

Growing up in Catholicism, Holy Week was a big deal. Jesus' death on the cross and resurrection were considered the holiest days of the year. Masses and catechisms preached there was power in shedding of blood. As my body grew into puberty and menstruation, then reproduction and childbirth, and moved into menopause, I felt a correlation with Christ's shedding of blood. Women's cycles emulating Holy Week, the life/death/life cycle of being broken and poured out. This is such a glorious image of female power. When women own their magnificent ability to shed blood and create, the revolution of sexual health will begin.

This cup is My blood, My new covenant with you, each time you drink this cup, come on and rise up and remember Me.

Female Orgasms

"The mind may be the ultimate sexual organ."

- Dr. Pauls

"So, are these my wild edges?"

Her ocean-drenched body looks empowered but cold as she emerges from the Strait of Juan de Fuca. The Pacific Northwest water is well under 60 degrees Fahrenheit when she asks me to baptize her. In the past, I would have cringed to think my client would ask me to submerge with her in the glacier water but I don't even hesitate at her request. I have learned the sacred act of a cold plunge. It takes mere seconds for me to wade into the frigid water and baptize her.

Baptism is the physical act of submerging under water to show the old life is gone and new life will emerge.

When she comes up, her native Florida body gasps from the full incantation. Her arms are shaking but she asks for another moment alone and I return to the beach. I watch as she requires her body to stay in the water and embody the moment. She baptizes herself once more before coming to the shore and grabs a towel and cradles her body to catch her breath. This will be the 18th woman that I will do a 3-day therapeutic intensive with this year. Each woman comes to bravely seek their own healing for their stories in hopes of regaining their voice, their self-awareness, direction in calling.

"Yes, these are what I call the wild edges of a woman. Each woman must learn to feel and see her own edge." I point to the jagged cliff that strikingly makes up this coastline we are standing on and I ask her to consider the water's edge as a guide. "Look at the ebb and flow of the water coming up on the land and then retracting. The moon guides the tide and these are often indicative of a woman's wild edges."

I have sat on this coastline for hundreds of hours watching the waters' relationship with the land. It often reminds me of the male and female energies; the masculine, strong rock beach and the free-flowing feminine water that both ebbs and flows. Some days, watching the waves crash against the rock shores demanding the ground to recede into the ocean mimics my own urging to shift the boundaries I feel. In my own relationship with men and society, I have had to explore my wild edges that come up against the boundaries set on women, particularly their sexuality. Every woman has her own wild edges, but often needs to be safe enough or mad enough to live out of them.

Do you know what your wild edges look like?

Much of my work as a therapist is working with women to integrate their stories and use their true voice into their everyday life. This work requires the female to find her wild edge and know it better than evil does. If we take my example of male and female energies, often in marriages, father-daughter relationships, or church relationships, the female represents the water's tide, while the male often presents more like the land, with its boundaries consistent and unmoving. The female must learn to trust her body as she leads her own life, and it will often follow an inner knowing that comes ashore and then recedes like the water's edge.

A woman's God-given body is her compass leading the ebb and flow of her wild edges.

If we consider female sexuality to the moon's tide. The arousal cycle of the female gives us insight to her wild edges. Science uses the term refractory period as the time following an orgasm when a person is no longer sexually responsive. For men, it is impossible to become physically aroused in the refractory period; whereas, for females, they may lose interest but they are usually physically capable of engaging in sexual activity again.

The female can theoretically orgasm as many times as she wants in her arousal cycle, whereas a man typically ejaculates when he orgasms leaving him without the possibility of another orgasm for at least 10-15 minutes. Scientifically, men haven't reported having orgasms more than 2 or 3 times during a sexual session whereas women have reported easily having 20 orgasms in a sexual session. Although it is easy for a female to have multiple orgasms, most of the female clients who have come to me report having one orgasm 20-30% of the time they have sex with their partners and their husbands having one orgasm 90-100% of those times. While this is not a statistic for all women, what does this discrepancy mean for these women's pleasure? If women can easily have 20+ orgasms during a sexual session, and many are not even orgasming once, I can only assume that women are not aware of their own sexual pleasure.

Often, women aren't having orgasms because they aren't aroused. There are multiple factors impacting female arousal, but we will focus on hormonal and genitalia in this essay. Through the lens of male sexuality, the female is conditioned to move quickly through arousal to climax and orgasm once. If we look through the lens of female sexuality, we must understand more about the hormonal cycle of the uterus. As mentioned in previous essays, typically, the female hormones run on a 28 day cycle sometimes referred to as each week reflecting: autumn (vibrant), winter (dormant), spring (awakening), and summer (passion). This is not true of every woman but can be helpful when women might find themselves more aroused in their spring and summer weeks due to ovulation or possibly less aroused during autumn and winter weeks due to menstruation.

In addition to a woman's brain and her hormonal cycle, there are two types of orgasms—clitoral and the g-spot orgasm. The clitoris has 8,000 nerve endings and is the size of an eraser tip. The penis has only 4,000 nerve endings. The clitoris has no other physiological function other than pleasure. An estimated 50-75% of women need clitoral stimulation to reach orgasm as they are not as likely to orgasm by penetration. As for the G-spot, it has been scientifically debated and many women report more success of clitoral orgasms than G-spot while some encourage simultaneous stimulation is most enjoyable. Yet all the information and techniques cannot compete with the sexual pleasure a woman can have with good self-esteem, healthy body image, a safe attentive partner, and no sexual shame. Why is this?

Because female's largest sexual organ is their brain.

Women have been taught to understand their sexuality through a male perspective, such a way of thinking might be, if the clitoris has 8,000 endings, we just need to rub it like a penis, and this will equal female orgasm. Yet that is a very simple and unhelpful want to understand female arousal. Researchers have come to find that for women the largest sexual organ is her brain, therefore Dr. Pauls concludes, if "the mind may be the ultimate sexual organ, which in combination with anatomy can augment sexual enjoyment". **Female arousal and orgasm is largely based on her mental state.**

This is all very good news for women and their sexual health. The female's story is her greatest sexual map. When a woman learns her story, understands her body, and develops her mind, she is on the path to sexual health. It is in this pursuit that she will learn to find her wild edges, and thus her sexual freedom.

Sexual Laws & Pleasure

"Sex is the woman's right, not the man's.

- Law of Onah

Doctors, therapist, parents, teachers, and pastors have trouble openly talking and teaching about sex. Universally, different cultures have different comfort levels with sexuality, but the Western, Christian culture is decades behind on sexual health research. Sex is a powerful and difficult subject to explore through the eyes of God, must less preach on it. Most churches have little education on who is equipped to navigate the conversations of sexuality and God, other than mandating abstinence. God's design for sex is obviously intentional and powerful, and I believe God has given us power in the act of sex and pleasure.

My professor and mentor for many years, Dr. Tina Schermer Sellers, is a Christian Certified Sex Therapist who trains Christian therapists on how to counsel clients around healthy sexuality[3]. She teaches about the history and practices of the Law of Onah, laws

---

[3] Sellers, Tina. (2017). Sex, God and the Conservative Church

directed mainly to men which command the man to give his wife pleasure during sexual acts, not to just think of himself[4]. Research records these laws from the Torah, specifically outlining a sexual principle that protects women as a direct rule[5]:

Sexual relations should only be experienced in a time of joy.

Sex for selfish personal satisfaction, without regard for the partner's pleasure, is wrong and evil.

A man may never force his wife to have sex.

Sex may never be used as a weapon against a spouse, either by depriving the spouse of sex or by compelling it.

It is a serious offense to use sex (or lack thereof) to punish or manipulate a spouse.

Sex is the woman's right, not the man's. Although sex is the woman's right, she does not have absolute discretion to withhold it from her husband.

Now whether or not you agree with these laws, we must ask ourselves, *"How did our traditional Christian sexual ethic diverge so dramatically from the attitudes and beliefs of our ancestors?"* and *"What happened in the development of the Western Church to evoke such a change?"*

---

[4] Nelson, 1999. Laws of Onah.

[5] Mamre, 2012. Torah 101: Kosher Sex.

As you read these teachings ask yourself how this is different from what you were taught about sexuality either by American culture or by the Western church. Can you see the relationship wisdom in these guidelines distilled over generations that increase the probability of a mutually satisfying sexual life for a man and for a woman? Certainly our Jewish ancestors provide us with plenty of food for thought.

Historically, the Vow of 'Onah is assumed by a Jewish man on the day of his wedding. This vow provides instruction on how he is to care for his wife. Here are some of the instruction in this sacred vow I want to expound on more:

Sex is considered a woman's right, not a man's.

Let's just stop there, I have NEVER heard that preached from a pulpit. EVER. Yet in Jewish law, the husband is given the commandment of 'Onah, which is one of the religious obligations he assumes at marriage, 'Onah is the commandment to supply all forms of well-being and pleasure to the wife. According to Hebrew scholar Moshe Idel, the term 'Onah as a religious obligation is not connected to the sexual satisfaction of the husband, but to the special sexual needs of the wife. The husband has a duty to ensure that all forms of sexual touch are pleasurable for her. He is also expected to watch for signs that his wife wants intimate touch and to offer it without her asking for it. Did you read that last sentence, "he is also expected to watch for signs that his wife wants intimate touch". Fascinating.

In the book Jewish Explorations of Sexuality, the author further expounds on the requirements of the husband to insure that all sexual touch be accompanied by closeness, *kiruv*, and joy, *simchah*. This level of attentiveness and intimacy raises love-making onto a higher, more emotional and spiritual plain. When we teach our children to construct a healthy sexuality, have we explained to them that it is a structure for emotional and spiritual intimacy as well as physical?

Sex and sexuality are not seen as primarily about genital intercourse.

All forms of sexual enjoyment are recognized from holding hands to sexual intercourse. Due to the lack of Eastern sexual education, we have deduced Kama Sutra, or the sexual positions as an understanding of sexuality. Actually, in some expressions of a Jewish faith, two weeks of every month were devoted to other forms of intimacy and intimate touch outside of intercourse. If we use Hollywood as a goal for our sexual life, we will only be aiming to simultaneously orgasm. What a simple, waterdown goal for the potential sexuality offers us.

The purpose in all sexual touch is to reinforce the loving bond and intimacy across the lifespan together.

Sexual touch is expected to evolve and change over time as life stages are lived together. Domesticated sex is a hardship on marriages that the law of 'Onah encourages us to explore our way through. The idea that an elderly couple is not sexually intimate is a foreign concept in the Torah context, because it is not limited to orgasm or intercourse. There is an invitation to make love to the same body through all seasons of life, scarred and broken or whole and healthy. The act of sex in aging is referred to by Dr. David Schnarch as "wall-socket" sex which can not be reached by a couple having only been sexually active for a short-period of time.

Sex for selfish personal satisfaction without regard for the partner's pleasure is wrong and considered evil. A man may never force his wife to have sex or use sex as a weapon against a spouse either by depriving the spouse of sex or by compelling it.

In Jewish custom, it is a considered a serious offense to use sex (or lack thereof) to punish or manipulate a spouse. Also, sex is not considered shameful, sinful or obscene. Lastly, I want to highlight this belief that "sex is not a necessary evil for the sole purpose of procreation. Some familiar with Hebrew scripture might point out sexual desire comes from the Yetzer hara, the so-called evil impulse, but it is well known by Jewish scholars that sexual desire is no more an evil impulse than the desire for food and water, which also originates from the Yetzer hara".

Sexual enjoyment is recommended for times when procreation is impossible, for example when utilizing contraception or during pregnancy.

Also, kosher sexual touch is not limited to behaviors that would lead to procreation, but extended to allow other activities if desired by both partners. Rabbi Moshe Feinstein wrote, "The duty of a man to engage his wife sexually is not contingent upon whether or not there is a the possibility of pregnancy, for it is mandated in the responsibilities of marriage that she should receive pleasure and not suffer, no different than the mandate that she be clothed and sheltered …"

The root word of sexuality is defined as meaning "to know".

Jewish scholars explain that the word written in the Torah for sexuality uses the root word Yod-Dalet-Ayin, meaning 'to know,' to describe sexual intimacy as a knowing of your spouse in mind, soul and body. Kosher research explains that the word "illustrates all sexuality, the act of knowing another in Yod-Dalet-Ayin, is meant to involve the whole of a person—the heart and mind—not merely the body. The Jewish understanding of sexual knowing and sexual sharing between a husband and wife took the whole person into consideration—heart desires, body desires, thoughts, feelings, etc. The body was not separated from the mind or heart. But this accountability to heart and mind in sexual intimacy was lost in the early Christian church translation when the focus of the term 'to know' became a negative expression condemning someone who had sexual intercourse out of the marriage context. This negative connotation is not in the original Hebrew meaning. The focus was a reminder of the importance of the mind and heart involvement in the sexual relationship".

We have much to learn from the Jewish laws of Onah which no where split spirit from body when it comes to sexuality, nor emphasize chastity as a sexual ethic. Our sexuality is a spiritual gift to know ourselves and another more deeply. We have deduced sexuality down to orgasms and sexual positions limiting the power and invitation healthy sexuality can offer.

---

[1] Kabbalah and Eros, Moshe Idel. 2005

[2] Jewish Explorations of Sexuality, Jonathan Magonet. 1995.

[3] Igrot Moshe, Even Haezer, Vol.1, No. 102. By Rabbi Moshe Feinstein

[4] Introductions to Judaism: The Source Book, Einstein, Kukoff, et.al. p114-122

[5] Judaism 101: Kosher Sex http://www.jewfaq.org/sex.htm

False Submission in Marriage

"The gift and responsibility of a relationship is to take turns doing the dishes and putting up the storm windows, giving the other a chance to dive for God without worrying about dinner.

While one explores the inner, the other must tend to the outer."

Mark Nepo

"Am I his lover or his mother?" I whisper to myself.

Most nights, I pick up around the house after my kids are asleep. The usual Lego pieces, dirty socks, and crayons remind me of the life that is lived in these walls, but too often, I also come across two or three pairs of my husband's shoes, clothes, and gym bags in some random rooms of the house. Upon picking them up, I sigh. I feel defeated and worried that he might never learn to pick up after himself. I internally blame my husband for his laziness or his own mother for never teaching him otherwise. I find my mind disappointed at his lack of discipline and my heart sad at how unseen I feel. I don't feel tenderness or sweet reflection as I carry his shoes to our closet.

Wives weren't meant to nag; they were meant to be lovers. Lovers aren't maids or enablers; lovers are pursued and respected. I was taught in the Protestant church that a woman was to be a helpmate. "Helpmate" is more commonly translated as a ***helper*** rather than a ***savior***. Either way, it has been communicated insufficiently from many pulpits. When we teach women to be silent, we fail to teach them *how* to be a savior or a helper in a relationship. Silent compliance leads to resentment and compliance leaves the other to become enabled. The enabled partner struggles to work hard enough to get everything out of life. I work often with spiritually abusive men who are not evil, but foolish. They are cursed because they do not understand or know how to get out of the entitled place they have found themselves in.

False submission is a term I have come to define after listening to too many disgruntled women who feel like they are staying silent in their marraige under the pretense that they don't want to nag their husbands. These women are having sex with their partners when they don't want to, they are not speaking up when they disagree, and they are hurting themselves under the lie that they don't want to hurt their husbands. Many silent wives become furious women hide behind the explanation, "I am submitting" when all along it is actually lying to themselves and growing contempt within their hearts.

False submission is silencing one's *knowing* self in the presence of the other.

My husband needs to put away his shoes, yes, but why is that so important? The answer is simple: my tenderness grows a little colder to him each time I don't require him to live out of his fullness. He is not a boy, he is not my child. He is a grown man, and my husband, and he can pick up after himself and our family. When I tiptoe around issues like this, contempt grows in my heart towards him. My failure is not keeping my heart tender enough for him to engage. I set him up for failure when I allow my heart to grow detached and dishonest. I fail him when I don't believe in him and require his best self from him. Now take the partner who is having sex when they don't really want to, wielding their body to open and receive their partner sexually when, in honesty, they have not desire to be sexually intimate. This kind of act is harmful, and will only ruin the trust in a relationship.

Resentment leads to contempt. My job in my intimate relationships is to guard my heart against contempt; that is my true role as a "helper/savior" wife. I save our relationship from the snares of distance, hardening, and keeping my desires from him. In my case of cleaning, I need him to pick up after himself. I need him to live out of his fullest self because it draws me to him. You may be thinking, "You are telling me that I have been doing this whole 'submissive wife' and Christian marriage thing wrong?" I am telling you that healthy, intimate relationships need honesty, growth, and risk to survive. When we silence the desires that are required for mutuality in relationship, we allow our partners to stay enabled. Honest relationships are made up of two people who both require and relieve each other.

Mark Nepo (2014) writes a beautiful metaphor about how the responsibility between pearl divers mimics the responsibility between a couple. He explains that for each pearl diver to be safe to explore the ocean floor freely, they must trust their partner to hold the oxygen line and count the time on the boat above. He explains, "The gift and responsibility of a relationship is to take turns doing the dishes and putting up the storm windows, giving the other a chance to dive for God without worrying about dinner. While one explores the inner, the other must tend the outer." His metaphor is so compelling to me as one who dives often, because the one who is on the boat courting the time must be trustworthy for their partner to dive safely and freely. The piece goes on to say that when the diver returns, the two sit for hours on the boat as they look through what treasures she found on the ocena floor. It won't be until the next day when the other diver take his turn to descend.

I think it is important to see that trustworthy lovers, not only protect their partner's space, but they spend time curiously listening to what the other found while they were away. In my marriage, when I leave for a trip, my husband stays home with our three kids and "counts the time" so to speak while I go away on my adventure. Not only is it important that he is trustworthy while I am gone, but when

I return or evenings at the end of the day, it is important to tell him all they ways my heart is coming alive while I am away.

The practice of sexual intimacy requires a similar balance of trust and responsibility. For intimate connection to thrive, we must take turns. One must be strong enough to enter while the other is soft enough to be entered. When I submit to a covenant relationship, it is my job to voice and require all that is needed to remain soft.

The greatest gift the submitted partner gives to their other half is to voice and require what they need to remain known.

Resurrecting Sensuality

"In short, I shall astonish you all."

- Bathsheba Everdene, Far From the Madding Crowd

In my quest to understand my own sexuality, I've come to find that I am not quickly aroused. What I mean to say is that it is the long pursuit that something awakens and arouses inside of me, deep within my core, deeper than my genitals. My husband asked me to explore my sexuality more. He was inferring that I might be curious about my body and my arousal cycle through the lens of only the genitalia, and in a sense, how I best come to orgasm. That exploration left me lacking in truly understanding or explaining my sexuality. As referred to in other essays, women's sexuality can not be explored using a male lens. For example, if women were to take the approach to orgasm as patriarchy does, simply stimulating the clitoris would lead the female to orgasm and be done. That is a masculine viewpoint to sexuality. For the female, her sexuality is comprised of the mind, which is her largest sexual organ; a woman's sexual story; the clitoris and g-spot, which is has over 8,000 nerve endings; and the female hormonal cycle.

The book *Far From the Madding Crowd* is the story of a relationship between two lovers who for years rarely physically touched each other. However, their commitment and banter within the ups and downs of life during the 1800s is deeply sensual and fraught with sexual tension and arousal. There is something of the cinematography of this lifestyle, horseback riding across farmland near the cliffs and ocean, that makes my body come alive. The story tells of a woman who is pursued by three suitors, which my stepdad would argue are the three types of male lovers in this world. I would argue his point. Either way, the woman in the story, Bathsheba, doesn't want a husband, as she states so boldly for the 1800's that she has no desire to be some man's property. The wrestling for equality in a relationship exposes different aspects of a female's arousal cycle. She is aroused by one lover who attempts to tame her, but the arousal is short-lived. Her long term arousal is awakened by a lover who is committed and consistent. I have come to find in myself and many of my clients that I can have a quick arousal cycle by what I cannot have, **the rebellious arousal**. This arousal seems to wane in domestication and over time.

The second arousal structure I am exploring is **the committed arousal** structure; to the partner that stays in relationship with me and stands by me through hardship and success. This is a more difficult arousal for me to feel. Quite often, female clients will get out of a relationship with a violent partner and will be attracted to similar men. Their work is often to date and find the care of what we jokingly call the boring partner. This is a person who is steady, faithful, and kind. This is a more difficult relationship to feel intense arousal. Longevity requires the hard work of commitment. Now that we don't live in the 1800s, the immediacy of technology hijacks our arousal cycles. Research shows us that the influx of imagery is not good for the brain's sexual development. In a society where digital information and media are bathing our brains with image after image, we stand little chance for healthy arousal structures. Women in particular are the teachers of baited breath in sexuality which often falls on issues of erectile dysfunction due to their partner's use of pornography. It is an uphill battle for many women to find and explore their sexuality much less the work of teaching and sharing it with their partner. Even I find myself jumpstarting the vulnerability required of me to remember the allure of a lover that remains to bear witness of the other through loss and accolades. The ebb and flow of two people who continue to seek and find the other. There are so many distractions, yet it is so much deeper than the sexual act—it is the sensual energy.

Bringing in the Five Senses

My colleague and friend Cherie Katt is a certified sex therapist. She begins all of her work with couples to explore the five senses whenever they are unpacking their sexuality and the health of their sex life. She remarked on the beautiful imagery that a couple is able to offer whenever they move into the five senses rather than staying focused on the act of intercourse. What does it mean to bring not only touch but taste, sound, smell, and sight into my arousal? Often my husband is aroused by sight and touch while I find myself in need of more—in need of poetry as my friend Steph puts it. I need all of it, the tension and beauty of nature, softness, emotion, and breath.

Sex is so much more than intercourse.

Sexuality is tightly interlaced with our sensuality.

My friends and I often laugh that during the first decades of marriage with children, our sexuality is often resurrected in places of warmth and vacation. For example, when my husband and I were away for one night in a hotel at the beach we had sex more times than we have ever had in a week in our Pacific Northwest home. Why tell you this? I need for myself to normalize that my sexual arousal is not fanned in a domesticated lifestyle. For myself, I find that energy comes for me either in rebellious arousal, such as a getaway night from the throws of normal life, or in commitment arousal, which awakens the longevity of loyalty and bearing witness to the other over the ups and downs of life. Sensuality allows for the other senses to participate with your sexuality.

Breath Work

There is a couple sitting on the floor in our office for an intensive counseling weekend. They are doing an exercise that involves uninterrupted eye contact and using incomplete sentences.

Each of them are sitting cross-legged and breathing in unison. As my husband and I lead them in the practice, they give one word answers to the sentences we invite them to finish.

"What I see in your eyes is"… *sadness.*

This scene is strikingly different from the 30 minutes prior when the couples were yelling at each other in rage.

I was on a walk with a few friends for a birthday celebration. The tide is low and we are able to walk a few miles along the train tracks. The rocks and shells are hard against our feet. We stop to notice starfish and sea anemones as we traverse this untouched ground. We are talking about this conversation of long winded sexuality and arousal to which one friend remarks that what you are talking about sounds like poetry, the desire to have the unseen collected overtime. As we walked back, the tide began to come in and we talked about the 14 feet of depth that is covered in the changes between low tide and high tide. The concept that so much depth and retraction can happen in such a short amount of time means within hours we can feel both filled and emptied. This resonates with my body with my cycles and even with my arousal.

"Love rests on two pillars: surrender and autonomy. Our need for togetherness exists alongside our need for separateness."

- Esther Perel, *Mating in Captivity*

Mating in captivity has led me to wonder if I will ever feel the same passion that I felt from my husband when I first saw him in the church foyer. He was wearing a crisp, white button down and although I was on the greeting team handing out welcome sheets, I actually turned and walked away, surprised by my attraction to him. Fast forward 13 years into marriage with three children, two miscarriages, and one stillborn child. Where is the man that I felt passion with? We enjoy eating ice cream and watching Netflix after the kids are asleep, but where is the arousal that physically wouldn't allow me to greet him. How can I explore and honor my arousal structure as an independent woman from the commitment of the man who stood by me and has not betrayed me when I have seen my lowest lows and my darkest days. Can I find a way to trust my fear and vulnerability in hopes that he will continue to remain, not only in loyalty but with the continued ask of my heart? Will he ask me again and again and wear down my stubborn heart that has grown cold and tired of him? I do not *want* to need him to ask me again, but I need him to.

Perel writes in her book Mating in Captivity, "Marriage is not the end of romance, it is the beginning. They know that they have years in which to deepen their connection, to experiment, to regress, and even to fail. It's a story that they are writing together, one with many chapters, and neither partner knows how it will end. There's always a place they haven't gone yet, always something about the other is still to be discovered."

In My Good Body

"The secret of health for both mind and body is not to mourn for the past, not to worry about the future, or not to anticipate troubles, but to live in the present moment wisely and earnestly."

-Buddha

I am moving through the class movements when I hear our instructor Anna say to the yoga class, "Relax your shoulders and pull your tongue back from the roof of your mouth." It takes a few seconds to register what she is saying and then I notice my tongue is in fact stuck to the roof of my mouth. I pull it back and coach my body to be in a more relaxed state. I look away from the mirror in front of me that accentuates a very unattractive part of my torso.

"Yes, Christy."

I am so deep in the uncomfortable yoga pose, I am not certain if Anna really said my name out loud. It is hard to believe that in the posh, downtown Seattle yoga studio filled with extremely fit, body-conscientious humans, she noticed my yoga pose and complimented it. It has been two years since I have been back to this studio, which I was a faithful weekly 6am Wednesday morning attendee for years before the pandemic hit. Today, I stare at my widened image in the mirror with grace. My pear-shape has matured and my thighs no longer allow light between them. I am not at home like I once was in my body or in my yoga practice.

I stare at my own sweat dripping on my rented mat. My son's Paw Patrol water bottle was all I could find in the car and I looked ridiculous next to the seasoned, much more stylish yogis filling the room. My legs are shaking as we push through a stretch from star pose through our vinyasa flow. Anna tells us to be kind as we finish our practice with an elongated hold. I have battled my negative body image throughout the entire practice and I push myself to hold the pose as long as I can.

"Good Christy."

She said it again. This time I'm certain Anna notices me amidst the entire class. Tears pool in my eyes as I lay down in savasana and I let myself feel her care. The strong ground holds me and my body melts into a rested breathing. I close my eyes and I never want to leave this moment. I just want to let Anna's mothering praise saturate into me. Anna finds me after class and asks me how it was. Tears prick my eyes again as I feel unusually seen and cared for; the vulnerability makes me aware of how empty I have been for so long.

A good teacher sees you and leads you, even when you don't know for yourself where you are. Anna's acceptance and praise of my imperfect body encourages me to be a kinder lover to my own body. As I spray my mat to clean it, I am taken by the drops of sweat my body spilled during this last hour. As if my body was shedding the shame and contempt that had collected onto me. I committed at that moment to be a lover of my own body, for she is a good body.

The aging and recovering body can often need more attention when it comes to sexual health. I have sat with disgruntled partners who are no longer attracted to the aging or sutured body of their partner. During my years working in the Oncology unit as a therapist, couples often came in with their broken sexuality, not knowing how to traverse mastectomies. Many men complained of being less attracted to their partner's scarred chest. I had to teach couples that their partner's scars were invitations into the most intimate places. We cannot look at the suture scars on a woman's chest as repulsive; we must see those scars as reminders that death did not take our beloved from us. **Husbands are invited to see that these battle wounds are intimate windows into their partner's soul.** Men can learn to kiss and bless the scars on the woman's body that victoriously prove that life will win. Whether it is scars from surgeries, from stretch marks, or from aging, these markers are gifts to the other lover of what real love is.

Often, we ourselves must first take in our own naked reflection and bless the scars that our bodies bear. The female must hold the complexity that her body was made to create life and that she will age and die. Some of the most beautiful parts of the female body get masked with reconstructive surgery or Botox which wipes away the body map of her story's closest encounters with death. The good female body, young and old, offers the world an understanding of God's beauty.

All My Naked Glory

"Here is my body, laid bare before you,

willing to be cut open so that life might be born.

I am a goddess, and this body will bring forth life.

I am naked, and I will not be ashamed."

Dr. Christy Bauman

The orange flammable soap suds bubble across my exposed abdomen as I lay on the operating table. The entire team of medics and the perinatal team are standing there in forced patience for three minutes waiting….

and I lay there naked,

waiting too.

Having had only vaginal births, I did not know the protocol for a C-section surgery. Wheel the hospital bed to the OR, put in IV, anesthetize, uncover the patient from the torso down, sanitize abdomen and then wait. I am aware that the surgical tech is the only male in addition to my husband in the room and I am instantly self conscious.

There is not a strong enough epidural to erase the inconsiderable feelings of laying here undressed and awaiting to be cut open. In all my years of counseling women in healthy body image, facilitating therapy for oncology patients awaiting surgery, this is my moment of personal schooling, my individual invitation to direct my anesthetized body to engage with what is about to happen.

My arms are both laid away from me with IV and monitors tapestried across both. From an aerial view my body is positioned in a cross-like form. I imagine Christ on the cross, I wonder if the cloth around his waist was really there or was His physical body exposed to the world.

The minutes feel unending as I wait naked and drying, so I muster a mantra in my head, anything to keep myself connected to this incredible sacrifice involved in birth. I can smell sterilization and I think about the act at hand, a scalpel cutting me open, and I begin to feel woozy. The medical staff is chatting quietly as if a woman lying naked, vulnerable and about to be spliced open is the most normal part of their day.

I focus on the male surgical tech, he is attentive to the tools on his small metal roller table. I feel ashamed that he is so close to the bottom of the table, near my exposed vagina. I coach myself to remember that I am about to offer the world a living human that I created inside of myself. I refuse to feel shame at this moment, so I begin to whisper my mantra aloud, *"Here is my body, laid bare before you, willing to be cut open so that life might be born. I am a goddess, and this body will bring forth life."* I say these words again just as I hear my doctor look up at the clock signaling the three minutes have passed, the orange sanitizing solution has dried and she say, "we are ready to begin".

A blue curtain is drawn between my chest and stomach, a pressure can be felt and I know they are going to get my little boy. It isn't more than five minutes before we hear his earth-awakening, premature cry erupt into the sterile and consecrated space. Undone by relieved fear, my husband and I break into deep cries of joy. We can not muster words, just overwhelming relief, our baby boy is alive.

There is life.

He is alive.

My naked body, torn open, has given way to life.

We are invited to see our bodies through a different lens, one that shows the naked body in its most vulnerable and bravest state. Every naked body bears glory boldly, and we must cultivate eyes that see this glory.

Long after my C-section scars healed, I sometimes trace my finger along the indentions on my lower abdomen and I bless the glory those scars bear. When my husband moves to kiss my scars, I feel elation that these scars bear our love's most glorious acts.

How do you see your naked body?

Can you bear the glory your nakedness bears?

PART 3:
Untangling the Sexual Lies

Entering the Sexually Wounded Place

"If anything is sacred, the human body is sacred."

-Walt Whitman

It has been three weeks since the D&C, there is little bleeding if any and I am crying in my husband's arms. The kids are asleep and we are attempting to have sex, but I can't stop crying. Sex is such an act of the present. My body and mind are timid and scared. My vagina remembers what my mind can't articulate, three weeks ago the pieces of our lifeless child were taken through this passageway and now my husband wants to enter this same place. Truly, this is not a moment I can explain completely yet my choice is to engage and share this deep sadness with myself and my partner or to silence this great grief and not offer him any invitation to intimacy. Sex is still such a taboo conversation in the church, yet there is such a power and holiness in sex that is not taught. When we offer our stretched skin, which we have carried all of our lives with us, and when we bring our history and ourselves to another person again and again we are invited into the holy of holies.

The holy of holies is the inner chamber of a sanctuary, separated by a thin veil. A place believed to be the most sacred and to be entered to receive atonement. I cannot prove that God made a woman's vagina to represent this concept, but there is something so sacred to be invited to enter into a person's body. I remember going into the hospital to birth my second child and my OBGYN wanted to try to break my water. She looked at me straight in the eyes, her lavender gloved hand ready, she said, "Christy, I am going into God's country now". I laughed out loud. Yet her words ring clear in my mind, there was a jovial honor that she was going to enter my body with reverence to check on the baby ready to be birthed. Her recognition, as a doctor, was that something divine had created my uterus and my vagina and it was a holy place. Our vaginas are not to be entered or engaged without honor and awe; it is an invitation to the holy of holies.

Sadly, I have the honor of working with many women who have had some type of sexual harm done to their bodies. Whether by childhood sexual harm, domestic violence, rape or trauma, I sit with hundreds of women who have received scars in the most sacred place inside of their bodies. Sometimes these memories don't surface until decades later when they are engaged in some type of physical act: sex, birth, a painful period, etc. Once these stories emerge we begin the process of psychological surgery in which we clean out a wound and re-suture. Our bodies want to heal and if we follow a few practices, our bodies will recover. This process can only be done when we honor our wounding by grieving and burying what has died. My husband and I were ambivalent around intimacy and pleasure during our grief; we had no guide on how to offer our traumatized bodies to each other in the holy and pleasurable act of sex. We had to first grieve together before we were able to find any pleasure in this sacred place. Sex needed to become something more than pleasure and an act of procreation, sex had to become the most powerful prayer where both grief and pleasure could co-exist.

The Differentiated Sexual Couple

"When I am not as angry as I should be,
I get angrier than I ought to be."

- My Therapist

I have been waiting for this wedding for decades. One of my dearest friends has met a good man and the entire sisterhood has been on our knees in prayer for the last three years that she would get to this day. Here we are, dancing in our dresses, childcare is covered, and my husband and I look amazing. Everything is perfect at this moment. Perfect, until my husband whispers in my ear as we dance that he is ready to go home. My heart sinks. I want to stay in this bliss all night. We barter for a bit until we reach a "30 minutes more" compromise. I am disappointed in my heart of hearts, but I acquiesce to the compromise.

This is a common predicament for us as a couple. Usually, it's on a Sunday morning after I've talked for over an hour with friends after church while he waits, frustrated and ready to go home to watch football. But how could he want to go home early tonight, of all nights? Doesn't he know how much this means to me? Doesn't he know how long I have waited to be in this moment? I want to bask in it. I want to watch my friend leave with her new husband; I want to be in the sending off pictures. I want the fullness of the experience.

We say our goodbyes on the dance floor and as I embrace my newly wedded friend, I can feel my annoyance towards my husband grow into anger. We get into the car and he begins to talk about how fun the night was and how he would love to have sex when we get home. I am starting to fume inside and the last thing I want to do is have sex. As we drive away, I feel like I am leaving my desires and my heart there at the reception and forcing my body to go home with my husband.

Why so much angst? Why can't I just let it go? I am not upset that he is tired and ready to go home; I am angry that I can't stand my ground and say that I want to stay. Our shared history is mitigating my desire to keep the peace. Often, I am the one to give in so that we don't have an argument or so that he doesn't get angry with me. What I am learning is that my silence sends me down a spiral of hiding and dishonesty by omission. As my therapist puts it, "When I am not as angry as I should be, I get angrier than I ought to be."

By the time we are home and have said goodbye to the babysitter, I am shut down and intimacy is eons away. This beautiful night feels tainted. My husband comments, "Just go back if you're this upset about it." I feel defeated. Even if I did go back, it wouldn't be the same. I want my husband to see how much it all means to me. I want him to want to share it *with* me. I want to be known and understood. I wish that I would have listened to myself, grieved that my husband wanted to leave, and used my voice to tell him I wanted to stay.

Jung refers to this as the individuated process, where one finds their individual self differentiated, and in this case, for example, me from my partner's self. Imagine that my husband came onto the dance floor and handed me a piece of cake which I didn't want. I could eat the cake because it was a kind gesture and then feel gross the rest of the night, or I could thank him for the gesture but refuse the cake. The second choice demonstrates healthy differentiation; I make the choice that is best for me and allow my husband to manage his own response to my choice. My husband wants me to tell the truth, even if it isn't what he wants to hear. When I silence myself because I don't want to upset him or I don't have the words to explain myself, then I will inevitably find another way to make him hear me ... usually a less healthier way.

Often with coupling, we lose sight of our individual self. Differentiation within a couple requires each to be actively in the ongoing process of defining self, revealing self, and clarifying boundaries. The differentiated couple must also manage the anxiety that comes from greater intimacy or potential separation. Individuation is a goal and often a lifelong process, time and time again we must hold onto our integrated self, recognizing our own uniqueness. Sadly, in intimate relationships I often find myself losing sight of my uniqueness and giving into what the other desires. This can happen easily for the woman who is not secure in who she is or her integrated self. This dynamic between my husband and I shows up in our sexual interactions also. It is important for a woman to check in with herself when it comes to her arousal and sexual desires so that she can offer her partner an honest invitation into mutual intimacy.

Blue Balled or Violet Vulvas?

"Although there is no scientific research to back it up,
women report physical discomfort when they are aroused but an orgasm
never comes."

-Dr. Teresa Hoffman

For a long time in our marriage, my husband and I would often check in with each other during climax. There were phrases like, "Can I go?" or "Are you close?" Even, "Oh man, are you done?" Whether we were in the dark and couldn't see the other's face or just uncertain of the other's experience, we had to check in on where we found ourselves in order to time simultaneous orgasm. The amount of disappointment or frustration one felt when the other climaxed alone was sometimes heart-wrenching in the early years of sex.

The differentiated self matters in sexuality, and it matters a lot. Many women sit in my office and tell me that they don't want sex because their husband will orgasm long before they are even close and they are left extremely frustrated. Women suffer from sexual frustration when they are aroused but not able to orgasm, but no medical or slang term exists for this experience.

Growing up in a Christian world where sexual frustration was a common occurrence since many chose to reserve intercourse for after marriage, the term "blue balls" was a widely understood phrase. Blue balls describes mild pain in the testicles from unrelieved sexual arousal. Many women experience this same frustration and discomfort, but without a term to use to explain it to their partners. Even more confusing is the sensitivity and shame that is often present in these conversations. But it is true; women can be blue vulva-ed or blue labia-ed or whatever term we might use.

In *Women's Health*, OB-GYN, Dr. Teresa Hoffman reported in an interview that,

> "Although there is no scientific research to back it up, women report physical discomfort when they are aroused but an orgasm never comes. Just like how blood flows to a penis when a person gets an erection, vulva owners get a similar rush when they become aroused. If they don't end up having an orgasm, there may be a tight, cramping feeling going on in there, which is pretty akin to what people feel in their testicles under the same circumstances. This feeling can last up to 20 minutes after the failed orgasm but typically resolves itself, even though you may continue to be emotionally frustrated."

This frustration may play a part in a woman's unconscious habit of avoiding sex with her husband. If she fears discomfort and unrelieved sexual tension, why even try? The likelihood of the man having an orgasm while the woman barely has a chance to even reach arousal is a roadblock to true and satisfying intimacy. This happens often, especially for women in a relationship with a man who suffers from premature ejaculation.

It is important in these situations to:

→ Have these conversations at the appropriate time.

→ Be aware of shame or self-contempt sneaking in for you or your partner.

→ Ask each other for help in the physical process of trying to connect intimately.

→ Remember that pleasure is not the only goal of intimacy, but it is an important one.

As you and your partner name and navigate these issues in your arousal cycles, it may be helpful to talk together with a marriage or sex therapist that can help you navigate your shared sexuality as a way to further your marriage's sexual health. There can often be a lot of hurt and rejection felt when these conversations are not navigated with care. There are a few intimacy exercises that can be used to encourage connection during intimacy.

→ Uninterrupted Eye Contact is the act of holding eye contact with your partner prior to foreplay or during climax and orgasm. This exercise can be helpful to track and match the arousal and connection between the couple.

→ Elongation of Male Arousal can be practiced by the female partner stimulating the penis on a scale of 0 to 10. The male partner lets her know when he reaches a 6 or 7 then stops climaxing. The partner then begins to arouse the male until he reaches an 8 or 9 and then stops climaxing. The man should not reach ejaculation and practice elongating his stamina of arousal.

→ The Yes, No, Maybe exercise allows one partner to touch every part of the other partner's body for about 5-15 seconds in which the person being touched responds "yes," "no," or "maybe" so that one's partner can learn what the other likes without taking the response personally.

→ The Body Blessing exercise is when one partner gets naked and allows their other partner to touch, anoint, and bless their body parts. This should be done in turns so that one partner gets the full attention for the evening and then the other partner has a turn the following evening.

Masturbating to the Glory of God

"There is only one logical answer to your question;
we must learn what it means
to masturbate to the glory of God."

- Dr. Dan Allender

Masturbation is a tricky subject in the Christian world.

Three hours have passed during his Faith, Hope & Love class lecture and I have barely noticed the time. The Seattle School of Psychology & Theology is a particularly special place for Andrew and me. The founder, Dr. Dan Allender, fathered us through our dating, engagement, and early marriage. The large classroom on the third floor of the brick building in downtown Seattle has held more tears, rage, and life-changing moments than any other graduate school building in the Pacific Northwest. Early in our engagement, I would sit in on Andrew's graduate classes because Dan was infamously known for his lectures on sexuality. Dan's lectures are a tornado of brilliance, nonsense, and conviction swirling through your body and brain, eliciting mind-blowing responses from his listeners.

The topic of sexuality and faith in this lecture, though I did not know it yet, would stay with me for the rest of my life. As the class neared its end, students were debating whether masturbation is permissible, beneficial, or sinful. The tense and heated argument felt like it had no right answer until Dan finished the class with these words: "There is only one logical answer to your question; we must learn what it means to masturbate to the glory of God. Class is over. I will see you all next week."

I will never forget that moment. I remember thinking as clear as day, *what did he just say?* Masturbate to the glory of God? We are standing there in a seminary and the moment felt so sacrilegious and holy at the same time. All of the students, even the ones still standing in heated debate positions, stopped in their tracks, both confused and dumbfounded.

Let's entertain for a moment that masturbation isn't an issue of right or wrong, rather an issue of the heart. Consider the clitoris again that was given to women with no other physiological function other than pleasure. Also, note that the clitoris is in a place on the body that doesn't require having another person to stimulate it. Lastly, ask yourself, what is God's intent for humans to experience pleasure? What would it mean to know God's desire for us to feel pleasure, even orgasm? Therefore, maybe our work in sexuality is to learn how to feel the pleasure of God's glory.

Masturbation is sometimes an act that young children do during the exploratory stages of development or a practice children use to self-soothe. Masturbation is a limited way to experience pleasure as orgasm in a relationship seems to be a deeper understanding of God's glory. The ultimate goal of sexual pleasure is to be enjoyed both individually and in a relationship. Masturbation is not the ultimate goal in sexual health and pleasure, yet how can we masturbate to the glory of God?

When we refer to historical sexual laws, the Law of 'Onah is a popular Jewish guideline for sexual relationships. As referenced in the sexual law essay, the first law as it addresses sexuality is that **sex must be experienced in times of joy**. Although these laws are referring to sexuality within relationships and we are talking about masturbation, I believe it is a helpful and fascinating rule for sexuality. If sexual pleasure is meant to be experienced in joy, we must also pursue masturbation in a time of joy. God created us to be in awe of His creation, particularly your good body that can feel pleasure as a gift given by your Creator who loves you and wants you to know you were made for love and to be loved.

When I work with couples, often the discussion of masturbation brings up distance and frustration. For example, a wife who felt overwhelmed with her husband's repeated requests for sex wanted him to masturbate so that she didn't feel so much pressure. When her husband would masturbate she would also feel distant from him but relieved at the same time. One practice I asked this couple to try was asking permission from the other to masturbate and to name the specific sexual memory they would use to masturbate to. This was an attempt for the couple to intimately connect by remembering and agreeing on the imagery of a sexual encounter from their past. When the couple practiced this exercise, the first two sexual memories the husband brought to his wife were actually unpleasant sexual memories for her. This sharing time gave the couple invitations to learn about each other and what was happening for them during an intimate memory. The wife took a turn to offer her husband a sexual memory when she remembered feeling beautiful and mutual; and the husband agreed and thanked her. He used this memory to masturbate to, and returned to talk with his wife about it after. They were able to connect and be intimate without actually engaging in intercourse.

This is one example of how to use masturbation in a healthy and intimate way. Sexuality is intended to produce intimacy and connection between couples. We must begin to be creative and curious about how to use sexuality in a healthy way that produces intimacy.

Sexually Transmitted Infections

> "If we base our self-worth on something
> as ever-changing as our bodies,
> we will forever be on the roller coaster
> of body obsession and shame."
>
> - Chrissy King

"I couldn't believe her when she came back in the room and said I had an STI."

Of all the things I imagined this client of two years might tell me in session today, it was not this. She is the most religious, straight-laced, virgin-like female I ever had as a client to date.

I kept my face poised and continued to listen. She explained that it was one night over a year ago with her boyfriend at the time. She had been so careful her whole dating life, never kissed or had sex with anyone committed to make it to marriage. Tears pricked her eyes at this part of the story, she put her head down and when her voice quivered the words tumbled out, "he told me he loved me and he wanted to marry me. I believed him. We started making out and he told me we should have intercourse to celebrate. I didn't want to but I didn't want to disappoint him. We broke up not long after that night when I told him I didn't want to have sex again because I wanted to wait until marriage."

It's quiet for a long pause and I imagine we are both aware that her ex-boyfriend gave her the STI and that she is now holding a lot of questions.

Did he know he had an STI when they had sex?

Was he sleeping with other people?

What does this mean for my future?

I picture myself protecting the space in the room, I want to keep any judgment or shame to enter the room. Any moment she will look up at my face to see what I think of her story. Tears pool in my eyes thinking about all she is holding.

She whispers defeatedly, "I feel like such a slut."

This is the greatest culprit of health, self-contempt.

Particularly when women begin to belittle their bodies and their sexuality, sexual health declines emphatically. Even though I don't believe this woman did anything wrong, she now contends with self-contempt rather than betrayal of her sexual partner.

The female's sexually story does not have much wiggle room. If she has been impacted by a faith culture or any culture of objectification, her sexuality is bound to her virginity. Fundamentalism suffocates understanding of Jesus' teaching about a woman's sexuality due to strict, male constructed beliefs that have been brainwashed by patriarchy and misogyny. As we talked about in other essays, sexual shame is defined as the belief that one's sexuality is wrong or bad. If a woman hears that her body can "make a man stumble" that she internally takes on the responsibility that her body and her sexuality is dangerous. Internalized sexual shame keeps women from developing a strong and healthy sexuality.

Furthermore, the female body is intuitive by nature. The hormonal cycle and lifespan of the female body all impact her sexuality. In psychology, the life cycle of the female uterus is used to explore health and well-being over the lifespan. There are three stages of the reproductive organs: adolescence (growing up and increased sexual drive), reproduction (peak hormonal time for pregnancy), and senescing (the decrease of hormones and growing down to menopause). The female hormone stages indicate the seasons of sexuality over the typical lifespan.

What informs the female's sexual health?

culture and family of origin beliefs,

hormone health,

sexual development story of individual.

My adult client had sex with her thought to be fiance once and got an STI. Now she sits in my office wondering how she will bring this conversation into future dating relationships and with her partner one day. Her body and brain have spent so much energy suppressing and fearing her sexuality, she has not had the freedom to develop a healthy sexual mindframe. For the first decades of her life she held the internal belief her body was dangerous sexually and now has an STI and carries a new, darker belief about being sexually "dangerous".

Her body is still good.

Her body was always good.

Her sexuality is still good.

Her sexuality was always good.

As her therapist, I will wrestle with doubts and fears to convince them of these truths, her body is good. Yet I won't be there when she looks at her reflection in the mirror, I won't be able to remind her that she is good. This will be her work, that she will bless her body and crawl out of the dark abyss of shame that she has been thrown into.

Monotonous Sex
Domesticated Sexuality

"The story of rewilding tells us

that change need not always

proceed in one direction.

It offers us hope that our silent spring

could be replaced by a raucous summer."

- George Monbiot, Feral

I hate loading the dishwasher but most nights around 9:15 pm you can find me in the kitchen filling it up and setting it to clean all night while I sleep. Deep in the futility of housework and parenting comes the satisfaction that my dishwasher will be working for me while I sleep. I don't mind cleaning dishes after a fun dinner party has ended but dread washing dishes for everyday mundane meals, smoothies crusted onto kids' cups, hummus blobs left on a plate, or mac and cheese dried on dishes left on the dinner table. Futility tries to swallow me up in its monotony.

I have almost forgotten that dinnertime was my favorite meal to prepare when I was on San Pedro Island. Actually in truth, dinner time was the *only* meal I would prepare for. At fifteen, long after my parents divorced, my time at my dad's house was spent practicing Spanish and diving for dinner. If you want to know how to catch lobster and make conch ceviche, I will tell you. As a teenager, I reveled in the fact that the meals I caught daily would have shown up as the most expensive items on a restaurant menu. Every day I was on the island, my father, siblings, and I would get on the boat around 11, and without exception, the clear blue ocean would greet me with adventure. My body felt alive and exhilarated by the task of fishing for my dinner. I practiced reading the water and watching the sway of the coral to know which way the waves were moving, much like an underwater weathervane.

A coral reef is the long strip of coral skeletons laid out across the ocean floor. When spear fishing, coral reefs are a compass to read the ocean. As our boat cruised along the crystal clear waters, I would watch with intent where the coral reefs would break. For a quarter mile or so, these areas leave barren patches of sand, and then you would see small rock piles where lobster might be hiding. After deliberation with my siblings, we would choose a spot. Once the anchor caught in the debris and sand of the ocean floor, the rocking of the boat would prove difficult for securing my flippers and loading my spear gun. This was a task I both loved and hated; pulling back the highly resistant gold rubber band to cock the spear in place could only be done against the strength of my thigh, usually leaving a bruise by the end of the day. My brother and I would usually team up, sitting on the opposite side of each other on the boat's edge, securing our masks, and falling backward into the welcoming water. Once under the water's cloak, we would swim to find rocks that might be hiding our sea crustaceans. ***The secret to hunting lobster is readiness.***

After a few hours of hunting these creatures in this repeated manner, we count our booty and I offer to seine on the ride home to gather enough conch to make up for what lobster meat we could not secure. If there are fewer lobsters caught, it is easy to make up for the meal with conch meat. My brother drives the boat home while I hold fast to the rope and seine the ocean floor for conch shells. This is one of my favorite pastimes letting the boat slowly carry me as I hang on to the rope being dragged through the water. I wear a snorkel mask which allows me to watch for small hidden mounds on the ocean's floor. When I spot one, I dive down and retrieve a conch shell to add to my wrist-held mesh bag.

Once docked and tied at home, we gather and shuck the conch with a screwdriver and knife while another sibling cleans the lobsters to grill. My body is exhausted from the hours of swimming, my sun-beaten skin salty. I feel the soreness in my muscles as I chop onions, tomatoes, and limes and hammer the conch meat. My siblings are all busy with the different tasks of cleaning food and preparing the meal. Music is playing; the conversation is full as we have spent most of the day surrounded by the silence of the ocean's white noise. These are the meals I was created to make; this is the cooking that makes me come alive.

These are my favorite dinners, the ones that I caught with my hands and churned into sustenance. The hunter and gatherer in me cannot find this same solace in ten years of making mac and cheese for my kids after a long day at work and then loading the dishwasher. It isn't enough to sustain the wild but domesticated heart. On these nights, after my kids are asleep and my kitchen is finally wiped down, I feel different exhaustion—*the exhaustion of domestication.* Although I am well aware that fantasy and wildness has a different cost and its own exhaustion, sometimes, I long for the days when my body feels full of sunshine and ocean rather than children's longing hands and loud thoughts. We commit to rootedness in order to offer the rhythm needed for procreation, but tucked inside of domestication my longing has become a grocery store aquarium of futility that requires more for me to flourish. Civility isn't enough to sustain this wild but domesticated heart. The truth is that domestication is lazier than the work of hunting, gathering, and living wild.

I turn off the kitchen light, toss in a dishwasher soap pod, and press the button three times by habit ... clean and soak cycle, high temp water, and delay two hours. I go to take my shower before the hot water is gone. Walking into my bedroom, I find a husband who wants sex while I feel no arousal whatsoever. Sex has become like loading the dishwasher.

The shower water reminds me of the ocean water I so often miss, and my mind wonders what it will take to ease the futility I feel in domestication without drowning in fantasy. Are you in a place of futility, domestication, or fantasy? Working with clients around domestication versus fantasy, I have come to notice the nuances between the two—*resuscitation is different from resurrection.* What does it look like to rewild domesticated sexuality? I don't want to go back to my single life, but I don't want to be shackled in my domesticated one—with myself, my partner, or God. I want to learn the art of resurrecting female sexuality.

If you have ever seen someone resuscitate a body, it is a harrowing experience. Manual labor breaks bones to force blood flow to pump through the veins. This is not the way we are to rouse the sexual self. The invitation of resurrection is more mysterious, nothing is forced but rather something awakens slowly. It begins with making space for curiosity. What does my body feel right now? *As I peek in the mirror to check for food in my teeth? As I brush past my partner in the kitchen? Does this sweater feel soft on my skin? These yoga pants feel comfortable and form fitting?* We begin to slow down to listen to our bodies and have an opinion.

Once we can hear what our bodies are saying to us, we pay attention. What does it need? As I explain in the essay, *The Construction of Sexual Health*, water and warmth are tied to my sensuality and moves me into sexuality. So, I find water at the end of an evening, as simple as a warm shower to help me feel my body again and awaken her.

Invite your body to be re-awakened to her healthiest sexual self.

Semen in my Underwear

"Embodiment is the female's compass in sex."

-Dr. Christy Bauman

"Ugh."

I am sitting in the toilet in the coffee shop bathroom looking at the semen on my underwear.

Today is not a day that I have time for semen. There is so much to do while my kids are at school, so many emails and phone calls to respond to, errands to run, and then with music and sports practices, I won't get home until late tonight. I don't have time for his semen.

Last night I had felt open to sex, even a bit aroused, but when I turned to initiate sex with my partner, he was snoring. Although my husband encourages me that if I ever want to sex, he is happy to be woken up, I turned over and went to sleep.

The next morning I found him reading in bed and he initiated intimacy. I was half asleep and not at all in the mood anymore. I also knew our kids would find their way into our bed at any moment and the pressures of the day capped any desire to open myself up to sex. One of my most coveted times of the day is when all three of our children cuddle together in our king size bed until we must break ourselves away to get ready for school. I didn't want to miss that opportunity this morning so the ideas of sex was more of a disrupting annoyance to my mental agenda.

My husband and I discussed the options. *Ugh.* Conversation about sex is very un-arousing to me. Already this deliberating pros and cons about trying to have sex annoy me and I find my clitoris imaginarily retract even further between my labials.

Because the bed is too easily accessible to a child's interruption we decide the shower is the best option. No interruptions, easy clean up, but less likely for me to orgasm. Once again, I check in with myself, expending my energy to keep frustration and futility at bay. This is not the tender grounds for great sexual encounters.

We shower and attempt foreplay but my mind is wondering about all I have to do today and if the kids will find our bed empty and begin their morning routine alone. My husband is aware of my distracted state and we decided intercourse is not for us this morning. We dry off and peek in our room to find our oldest snuggled in our bed. Excitedly, my husband and I both dry off, dress and jump back into bed to chat with him about his night sleep. More kids follow, and we begin our day with sacred family connection. My body and mind relax.

We all talk about our dreams the night before, while different birds congregate at the bird feeder outside our bedroom window.

We discuss the schedule of the day and then the kids run off to dress and eat breakfast. I smile at my husband and he says, "I love our family…do you want to have sex really quick?" Before an immediate no, I check in with myself, and surprise to find that I sort of want to have sex. Somehow the remaining hormones from my arousal the night before linger and I hesitate still to answer. My body does want sex but my schedule does not. The logistical facts flood my brain, we need all five of us to be out the door in the next 15 minutes. Usually that is a terrible recipe for sex, but today it isn't. We quickly make love, both successfully orgasm, and hurry to dress for the day. I have a bit of a rule with quickies, I won't do them more than three times in a row without a solid, good, long act of sex. Quickies are not my favorite way to orgasm.

My husband gets the kids in the car while I clean up from sex and attempt to pee even if just a little. The fear of a UTI runs strong in my female lineage and peeing after sex is a common rule where I come from. I turn my mind toward getting myself out the door. It won't be until two hours later that I feel the sensation of liquid pouring down. I quickly try to make it to the coffee shop bathroom but sadly I never make it in time. Semen is my arch nemesis when it comes to efficiency.

I stare at it, having soiled my clothes and then exhale my frustration. Why does sex require so much from the heterosexual female? My husband doesn't spend the next 24 hours after sex cleaning up from it. The mere physiological fact that the woman

131

must be entered shows the extra energy that female must take on when having sex with a man. Then we add the extra hormonal energy it takes for the typical woman's arousal cycle to reach orgasm, and I'm already exhausted thinking about it.

Futility. I hate futility.

Domesticated sex invites me into making meaning within futility. So I can look at that semen in my underwear and internally respond in many ways.

Annoyance. Futility. Brave. Committed. Love. Inconvenienced. Tamed. Rewilded. Hopeful. How will I see the semen in my underwear? As a win, a check off my checklist, a nuisance, a sacrifice?

The work of the female arousal cycle has been complex at best for me. She is specific to our biology and physiology. She has two places for orgasm, clitoris and g-spot. The female can attain multiple orgasm in succession while the male can only attain one at a time. In these areas, the female body is equipped with a double capacity for pleasure than the male yet often more is required from the female body to reach arousal and orgasm. This is why in Greek and other mythologies the female arousal cycle is the pathway to the divine. Men were taught that bringing a woman to orgasm would teach them how to attain true divinity.

Say what?

It is believed that when opposite genders meet in the perfect connection, the divine is reached. Where typically a male orgasm can happen quickly and once, the female invites him to elongate his arousal cycle. While the male's arousal invites the female to awaken her desires and thus the couple can enjoy multiple female orgasms which provide infrastructure for the male orgasm.

Basically, the female arousal cycle hugs the male arousal cycle and slows him down to enjoy as much of the connection as possible and ultimately as long of an orgasm as possible. To do this, the female must be in her body, or it is commonly referred to as embodied. Embodiment is the female's compass in sex.

Our physiology obviously plays a huge part in sexuality, but I would argue our stories a significant part as well. It matters if our bodies hold stories of sexism, objectification, patriarchy, or misogyny. Our physiology and psychological bodies impact how we come to hope, longing, desire, pleasure, and these are key factors in sexuality. Female bodies that have been impacted by sexual harm may struggle to lead male arousal cycles during healthy sex. Women must know their own sexual story, and must learn their arousal patterns.

I have come to this conclusion again and again in my sexuality, to the level I want to engage in ecstasy, I must engage in grief. The elongated lifespan of female sexuality (see more in my essay Theology of the Womb), specifically adolescing, reproductivity, and senescing, invite me into the same pathway to the divine. It is the same as attaining multiple orgasms, I must hold the capacity to engage in the highest highs and the lowest lows. This is grief and ecstasy.

This is one plight of female sexuality.

Sex as Prayer

"Loving yourself is the greatest revolution."

-Unknown

Amen, and let it be.

This is often how I end my prayers. And sometimes, after the work of connecting with my husband and engaging in sex, how I end my orgasm. *Amen, and let it be.* As a trauma and abuse counselor, my job is to dissect stories of sexual harm and abuse. I spend my days at work with a figurative scalpel and suture kit as I extract and mend stories of sexual hurt and objectification. Stories of sexual abuse and objectification have cost my sympathetic system years of damage. Honestly, I would give up sex in a millisecond if it could heal and stop all the sexual harm this world has encountered. Yet, God created sex knowing it would also cause so much harm. This baffles my mind and also challenges me to consider what God intended sex to accomplish for good. If God made sex, I deduce that it has to have a stronger superpower than what evil has used it for.

So what was God's intention for sex? Procreation is a common answer. But what about those who desire to create and yet are not able or do not want to have children? The power of what we can create together with another being in sex is absolutely mind-blowing. My husband and I set an intention when we have sex. For whose sake are we engaging in this act? Sometimes we literally say, "*We consecrate this time of sexual connection to combat evil in this world.*" If part of our glory occurs when we engage in a covenant with another, with integrity and vulnerability, and we receive pleasure—well then, let the sexual creations come! Let us offer our scared and wounded bodies to the other in an act of faith that God will show up and bless each other with pleasure and a taste of heaven.

Growing up in the church, no one told me very much about how to navigate sex as a Christian woman. Truthfully, I did as I was taught and stayed a virgin until marriage, praying that would secure a healthy sexual lifetime for me and my husband. *I wish it had been that easy.* Why didn't anyone explain that sex is a powerful tool in the kingdom of God? So powerful that evil has used it to harm countless numbers of people. Shouldn't that mean God intended it for something extremely powerful?

The laws of Onah that I spoke about earlier in the book invite us to begin the exploration of God's design for sex as it relates to pleasure and spirituality. It was during my first seminary class discussion that my professor mentioned that the female clitoris is the size of a pencil eraser head, but has more nerve endings than the head of the male penis. I was shocked; no one had ever told me that. She posed the question, "Why would God give women a clitoris which only has the physiological function to give pleasure?" I researched the function of the clitoris, finding it described as an extremely sensitive organ made up of erectile tissue which has thousands of nerve endings, with its central function being to produce sensations of sexual pleasure. I was stunned to confirm that the clitoris, in fact, has no function in reproduction and has 8,000 nerve endings, which is double the amount of nerve endings on the penis.[6] *Who knew seminary could be so helpful?* This information has been a stunning revelation for thousands of students and clients that I work with. We are under-educated as a Christian population about God's design of the female body, especially concerning sexuality. How can we expect to build a healthy theology around God's plan for sexuality if we don't study His design of our sexual organs?

Objectification of the female body brings death. If a woman's reproductive, life-creating body parts created by God's image are objectified, it prevents her body from being engaged with in the way God intended.

Rob Bell describes Christian sexuality as a dance between being "angel," a spirit without a body; or "animal," a body that lives by basic instinct. Bell writes about how we, as believers, must live as human, neither angel nor animal, but somewhere in between:

---

[6] (Madsen, 2016).

"Angels were here before us. Animals were here before us. When we act like angels or animals, we're acting like beings that were created before us. We're going backwards in creation. We're going the wrong way ... our actions, then, aren't isolated. Nothing involving sex exists independent of and disconnected from everything around it. How we act determines the kind of world we're creating. And with every action, we're continuing the ongoing creation of the world. The question is, what kind of world are we creating? How we live matters because God made us human. Which means we aren't angels. And we aren't animals." (Bell, R. 2007, p.63-64)

The question he asks is applicable to every person at every juncture of life: What kind of world are we creating? In the context of our sexuality, we must ask ourselves this question. Do we see sexuality as something to fear, or have we trusted that God created sexuality as a powerful tool for creating? How do we use our sexuality for the glory of God? How do we use our bodies for creating? The secular culture leads us to believe that we are animals (i.e., over-sexualized) and often the church leads us to believe we are angels (i.e., asexual). In particular, the woman's body through pregnancy demands us to see that sex is designed to create life.

What kind of world are you creating—one of objectification or true intimacy? Our sex life is a powerful prayer telling the story of who we believe God is and who we believe God created us to be.

What kind of world are we creating as Christians? I think the answer is displayed in our sex life.

If you are curious about what this looks like, invite your partner to pray before sex and begin to explore what God might show both of you as you reflect on His intention for your intimacy. Whether you intentionally ponder these things in your prayer time alone or together with your partner, God is ever present and ready to bless the prayers for your sex life. May it be so.

Conclusion

L ast year, I drove cross-country twice with my husband and three children. There is a lot to say of the places we visited driving from the East Coast to the West Coast in over 100 degrees Fahrenheit and then six months later in below freezing temperatures. Yet the mountain ranges remained the same whether covered in dry, barren terrain or crisp, chilling blankets of snow.

How does this conclude this book on sexuality?

What I observed during both drives were the change of landscapes, particularly the mountain ranges. The Pacific Northwest mountain ranges were sharply masculine in their stature, jagged and gray; as if my own adolescent testosterone dared me to take them on and summit their peaks. The older, worn down Smokies and Applachians are rolling in nature, as if all of my grandmothers and great mothers laid down and their chests and hips invited me to hike them. Both the masculine and feminine energy invite us to understand that sexuality is an integration of these two for a moment.

The feminine and the masculine energies are in all of us, and we are opposed and drawn to them both at different levels. Our arousal toward them changes with temperature and time. Just as we are

141

cyclical so is our sexuality. It is important as you finish this book to understand these are nothing more than reflections of sexuality and stories of sexuality from a mental health therapist and a God-loving woman. Take these stories and hold the ones that are helpful to your journey, and forget the ones that are not good for your health.

You are a sexual being, made in the image of your Creator. You were given sexuality as a tool, both powerful and vulnerable. One thing your sexuality must have to be healthy, is that your sexuality is yours and yours alone. You share it with only who you want.

To you, and your sexuality. May you be well in the good body you have been given.

About the Author

D r. Christy Bauman, Ph.D., MDFT, & LMHC is committed to helping women come into their true voices. She has a podcast entitled Womaneering and she offers story-work consulting, womaneering weekends, and marriage intensives with her husband Andrew Bauman through their organization, Christian Counseling Center for Sexual Health and Trauma. Andrew and Christy host the Therapy Shorts podcast for couples. She is the author and producer of her works: Theology of the Womb, Womaneering Perpetual Calendar, A Brave Lament, and the award-winning Documentary: A Brave Lament. She is a psychotherapist, supervisor, and part-time professor who focuses on the female body, sexuality, and theology. Christy's work can be found at christybauman.com, she works between her Asheville, NC and Seattle, WA locations

Made in the USA
Monee, IL
14 March 2023

29872039R00089